# TOUCHING

# FIRE.

# TOUCHING

# FIRE

## EROTIC WRITINGS BY WOMEN

Edited by Louise Thornton,
Jan Sturtevant, and Amber Coverdale Sumrall

Carroll & Graf Publishers, Inc.
New York

Copyright © 1989 by Louise Thornton, Jan Sturtevant &
Amber Coverdale Sumrall

First Carroll & Graf edition 1989

Carroll & Graf Publishers, Inc.
260 Fifth Avenue
New York, NY 10001

Library of Congress Cataloging-in-Publication Data

Touching fire: erotic writings by women / edited by Louise Thornton,
Jan Sturtevant, Amber Coverdale Sumrall. — 1st Carroll & Graf ed.
    p.    cm.
  ISBN 0-88184-527-2 : $18.95
    1. Erotic literature, American—Women authors.   2. Women—Sexual
behavior—Literary collections.   3. American literature—20th
century.   4. Erotic literature—Women authors.   I. Thornton,
Louise.   II. Sturtevant, Jan.   III. Sumrall, Amber Coverdale.
PS509.E7T68   1989
810.8'03538—dc20                                                    89-37987
                                                                        CIP

Text designed by Terry McCabe

Manufactured in the United States of America

For Audre Lorde
Who Ignited the Flame

We wish to express our deepest appreciation to our agent, Charlotte Raymond, for her spirited work and unfaltering faith in this book. For his good humor and conscientious attention to detail, we wish to acknowledge our editor, James Mason.

For the continuing support, love and encouragement of the women in the Santa Cruz writing community, we are ever grateful. Finally, we would like to thank the contributors themselves for their eloquence and for their commitment to a new definition of the erotic.

Acknowledgments:

**Deborah Abbott:** "This Body I Love" originally appeared in *Matrix Newsmagazine* and is included in *With The Power Of Each Breath: A Disabled Women's Anthology* (Cleis Press) copyright 1985. Reprinted by permission of the author.

**Elisa Adler:** "Let's Make Jazz" originally appeared in *Arc*. Reprinted by permission of the author.

**Ai:** "Why Can't I Leave You" reprinted from *Cruelty* by Ai, copyright 1970, 1973. Reprinted by permission of Houghton Mifflin Company.

**Renee A. Ashley:** "Rocking" is an excerpt from the novel, *Someplace Like This*. Printed by permission of the author.

**Margaret Atwood:** "Late August" reprinted from *Selected Poems 1965–1975* by Margaret Atwood. Copyright 1976 by Margaret Atwood. Reprinted by permission of Houghton Mifflin Company, Oxford University Press, and Phoebe Larmore.

**Ellen Bass:** "If You Want Me" reprinted from *Of Separateness & Merging* (Autumn Press) copyright 1977. Reprinted by permission of the author.

**Maureen Brady:** "Care In The Holding" originally appeared in *Feminary,* Spring 1985 and is included in *The Question She Put To Herself* by Maureen Brady (Crossing Press) copyright 1987. Reprinted by permission of the author and Crossing Press.

**Beth Brant:** "A Simple Act" reprinted from *Mohawk Trail* by Beth Brant (Firebrand Books) copyright 1985. Reprinted by permission of the author.

**Anne Cameron:** "A Bear Story" reprinted from *The Annie Poems* (Harbour Press) copyright 1987 by Anne Cameron. Reprinted by permission of the author.

**Naomi Clark:** "The Ring-Necked Snake" originally appeared in *Cimarron Review,* January 1989 in a different version titled "The Language of Doors" and is included in *When I Kept Silence* by Naomi Clark (Cleveland State University Press) copyright 1988. Reprinted by permission of the author, Board of Regents of Oklahoma State University and Cleveland State University Press.

**Lucille Clifton:** "homage to my hips" is reprinted from *Two Headed Woman* by Lucille Clifton (University of Massachusetts Press) copyright 1980. Reprinted by permission of the author and University of Massachusetts Press.

**Gina Covina:** "There Are Flowers For Everyone In These Hills" is a chapter from the novel, *The City of Hermits* by Gina Covina (Barn Owl Books) copyright 1983. Reprinted by permission of the author.

**Rosemary Daniell:** "Talking of Stars" reprinted from *A Sexual Tour Of The Deep South* by Rosemary Daniell (Holt, Rinehart & Winston) copyright 1975. Reprinted by permission of the author and Wendy Weil Agency.

# Contents

Introduction
  Louise Thornton                                    1

**Part I. Rousing the Waters**                      13

Baptizing
  Alice Munro                                        15

Twilight
  Doreen Stock                                       17

The Secret
  Janet Aalfs                                        19

from: The Heart of the Fire
  Cerridwen Fallingstar                              22

from: Their Eyes Were Watching God
  Zora Neale Hurston                                 25

Paper Boy
  Amber Coverdale Sumrall                            27

First Sex
  Sharon Olds                                        31

I Am Horny
  Susan Lysik                                        32

Re-Forming the Crystal
  Adrienne Rich                                      35

Womantides
  Amber Coverdale Sumrall                            37

ix

Touching
  Terry L. McMillan                                              38

Kalaloch
  Carolyn Forche                                                 46

Moving House
  Patrice Vecchione                                              49

The Game of Chess
  Sandy Boucher                                                  50

Talking of Stars
  Rosemary Daniell                                               59

Eros
  Yuri Kageyama                                                  60

New Mother
  Sharon Olds                                                    62

Domestic Love
  Jill Jeffery Ginghofer                                         63

Beginning to Love Again, in the Middle of My Life
  Carol Staudacher                                               67

from: Winter's Edge
  Valerie Miner                                                  68

Shih Ho: Biting Through
  Flora Durham                                                   72

**Part II. Rocking the Earth**                                   73

May Day
  Judith W. Steinbergh                                           75

Let's Make Jazz
  Elisa Adler                                                    76

There Are Flowers for Everyone in These Hills
  Gina Covina                                                    77

This Year I Can't Complain
  Irene Marcuse                                                  79

Frontispoem: Lost Copper
  Wendy Rose                                                     80

The Privacy of Corn
  Ann Zoller 81

An Encounter in Muse, Pa.
  Helen Ruggieri 84

A Bear Story
  Anne Cameron 87

Desire
  Florinda Colavin 88

What Will We Do About Angus?
  Eva Shaderowfsky 89

Ovation
  Deena Metzger 95

Wolf Man
  Clarinda Harriss Lott 96

After Love
  Maxine Kumin 97

This Body I Love
  Deborah Abbott 98

Homage to My Hips
  Lucille Clifton 101

On Second Thought
  Maude Meehan 102

Late August
  Margaret Atwood 104

Careless Love
  Louise Thornton 105

**Part III. Touching Fire** 117

Rocking
  Renée Ashley 119

Moon in Taurus
  Deena Metzger 122

The Coyotes
  Deborah Abbott 124

Lot's Wife
Nancy Redwine                                          127

Rain Tree
Jan Sturtevant                                         128

China
Dorianne Laux                                          129

It
Sharon Olds                                            130

Where We Are Now
Cathryn Alpert                                         131

Piñata
Kathy Metcalfe                                         134

from: Zami: A New Spelling of My Name
Audre Lorde                                            136

Porch Lovin
Judith W. Steinbergh                                   149

The Laundromat
Dorianne Laux                                          150

The Triangle
Patricia McConnel                                      151

Under Red Aries
Marge Piercy                                           157

Why Can't I Leave You
Ai (Florence Ogawa)                                    159

**Part IV. Restoring Spirit**                          161

Stephanie
Joan McMillan                                          163

Star Quilt
Roberta Hill Whiteman                                  164

Snow in May
Marge Piercy                                           165

Siesta
Amber Coverdale Sumrall                                166

Hair
  Enid Shomer                                     169

A Simple Act
  Beth Brant                                      170

The Ring-Necked Snake
  Naomi Clark                                     173

The Natural Lover
  Jill Jeffery Ginghofer                          175

Do You Know the Facts of Life?
  Lynn Luria-Sukenick                             177

Afternoon Poem for a New Lover
  Susan Lysik                                     186

If You Want Me
  Ellen Bass                                      187

Care in the Holding
  Maureen Brady                                   188

To the Angel
  Abby Niebauer                                   197

Elizabeth and William
  Heather Grey                                    198

Each Bird Walking
  Tess Gallagher                                  205

Out of Darkness
  Amber Coverdale Sumrall                         207

Afternoon I Almost Left You
  Abby Niebauer                                   208

Of Gravity and Angels
  Jane Hirshfield                                 209

Biographies                                       210

# Louise Thornton

# Introduction

*A memory: I am four years old and staying at my grandfather's farm. The barn is fragrant with the sweet smell of clover, and my grandfather, who is milking a cow, sits on a low, three-legged stool, his head turned so that one cheek almost touches the cow's smooth side. "Do you want to try it?" he asks. I nod yes and he takes my hands and folds my fingers around the soft, warm teats. "Oh . . ." I giggle. "They're so squishy! I don't know if I can make them work."*

*"Just squeeze," my grandfather urges, "but not too hard. You don't want to hurt her." I imitate the rhythm of his hands: squeeze and pull, squeeze and pull. A thin stream of creamy milk splashes into the mottled tin bucket. "Fine! Fine!" my grandfather assures me. As I release my fingers, my grandfather's brown hands circle the pink teats, and the milk continues to drum against the bottom of the pail.*

*The barn cat wanders in and stands beside the stall, mewing plaintively. "Come!" my grandfather calls. The cat runs under the udder, opens her mouth, and licks greedily as my grandfather squirts the milk directly into her mouth. I imagine that I am the cat, sweet milk pouring into my mouth. My grandfather continues to squeeze the swollen teats until they are flaccid. In the darkness we walk together across the yard where light from the house falls across the grass in golden swaths. I am complete.*

This anthology celebrates the sense of union with all of life that I knew then. It praises response: a hand slipped into another for the first time and held firmly, a quickening of the breath, almost a fear of breathing as the body takes in this pleasure of palm against palm. It honors trust: the giving of one mouth to another, breasts to tongues, hands to openings, momentarily surrendering all that one is to the other.

Yes! it says to sensuality: play of light on the contours of the buttocks, play of tongue on skin, hands stroking the

1

sinuous line of the thigh with tenderness and grace. Yes! it says to desire: ache for the touch of a lover, wanting beyond all sensibility, waking and reaching for the arms of the other, fires burning through the night. And yes! it says to passion: opening of the body, open mouths, hearts pulsing fast and open.

In the soft flesh of the body, in the pleasures of sensuality, in our feelings and in all of life is eros, the powerful, often unconscious force that permeates our lives. "It (eros) is constantly cracking open the heart and pulling us off in directions where we lose conscious control. Sappho writes in one of her poems: 'Love shakes my heart like the wind shaking the tree.' Eros is like that—a shudder to the whole system, an uncontrollable, unpredictable movement."* Without this force our lives might be completely stable, orderly, and secure, but our lives would also be cold and barren. This anthology, then, celebrates the inherent and life-affirming place of eros in women's lives.

The erotic is intrinsically connected to the very essence of the lives of women. In Audre Lorde's essay, "Uses of the Erotic: The Erotic as Power," she states: "The erotic is a resource within each of us that lies in a deeply female and spiritual place, firmly rooted in the power of our unexpressed or unrecognized feeling . . . [It is] an assertion of the life force of women; of that creative energy empowered, the knowledge and use of which we are now reclaiming in our language, our history, our dancing, our loving, our work, our lives."** It is this concept of the erotic that Amber Coverdale Sumrall and Jan Sturtevant and I employed while compiling this anthology.

The word *erotic* has as its root the Greek word *epws* which means love of all kinds including, but not limited to, sexual passion. Eros, the god of this all-encompassing love, was the son of Aphrodite, the goddess of love and beauty. In her earlier form she was Isis who described herself so: "I am Nature, the Universal Mother, Mistress of all the elements, primordial child of Time, Sovereign of all things spiritual, Queen of the Dead, Queen also of the immortals, the single manifestation of all gods and goddesses that are." (*The Golden*

*Susan Griffin. "Women, Nature and the Denial of Eros." Yoga Journal Jan./Feb. 1988:86.

**Audre Lorde. Sister Outsider. Trumansburg: The Crossing Press, 1984, pp. 53–55.

Ass, Apuleius) Thus eros is the child of the spirit moving through all and in all. The erotic is, as one of our contributors, Deena Metzger, wrote to us: "Everything in service of the life force." It is all that keeps us desiring to be alive.

When we abandon ourselves to the rhythms of a dance, gaze at the stars, or stroke a lover's face, we are one with eros. The stories and poems that make up the body of this work reflect women's experiences as they praise the erotic and its power of transformation in all aspects of life.

The selections included were chosen from submissions we received after placing requests in women's newsletters and periodicals. After many pleasurable hours spent reading the work sent to us, we selected writings rich in sensuality and desire: "He lays her down / fills her mouth with his tongue / only tiny vowels escape from her throat / She feels her back lengthen under him / each cartilage opening like a flower / on her spine." ("Piñata," Kathy Metcalfe). This unfolding is also a theme of Irene Marcuse's poem: "I'm open, open / The moon swells / Can't close myself."

Judith Steinbergh's "Porch Lovin" reiterates this theme: " / Before I blink you're naked on the / porch, your freckles low under the street lamp, / your cock nodding stiffly in the warm air. Hello, / it might be saying to the Silverman's daughter / just returning from the Cape, but it is too busy in / me now speaking to that other darkness." The trust of this man standing naked in the pale light says: it is all right to be this exposed. The essence of eroticism, then, may lie in this willingness to be vulnerable within a life-affirming context.

The erotic, neither trivialized nor degraded but allowed to be as pure and elemental as an ocean wave, is almost always sensual. It is, as the writer Anne Cameron described to us: "The muscles rippling in a woman's back as she hauls and stacks winter firewood; tanned skin dusted with garden dirt, the smell of moss and leaf mulch, the smell of an ocean after a storm, my beloved's hands. . . ."

Deborah Abbott writes of the pleasures of the bath. "Oh, and the lovely left arm still raised, suds careen down the slope of breast, heap on my nipple like cream on warm pie, then edge over, splatting the tile. Such fondness I have for these breasts . . ." ("This Body I Love") And in "Womantides" Amber Coverdale Sumrall states: "I want the swell of your hands / beached deep inside me / the slow lap of your tongue." Erotica "seduces the reader with the rhythms of sensual experience" (Renée Ashley).

As we organized this anthology, it fell almost effortlessly into sections honoring the elements ruled by Isis/Aphrodite and inhabited by Eros: water, earth, fire and air/spirit. In the first section, "Rousing the Waters," we focused on the initial stirrings of the erotic. These stirrings speak of the feelings for which we have no name, lying in bed, our hands of themselves nestling between our legs, touching again and again. They speak of the slow descent into oblivion the first time we kiss a lover on the mouth in a long falling, all boundaries left behind except the tongue and endless pink cavity of the mouth. And they speak of the heightened sensitivity of skin as if it never before existed until touched by fingers caressing nipples or tracing the soft curve from hip to groin, all alive with desire.

"Rocking the Earth," the second section, pays homage to the sense of sound: rain drumming the earth, drumming the windows, small love cries rising above the drops of water splashing against the glass. It praises the smell of clean hair, smell of the beloved after making love, smell of clover floating above a drowsy field, smell of hibiscus. It celebrates lips, shoulders, the hollows alongside the thighs, all the soft places of the body, no hardness, no bone, yielding. It lauds "Fullness between my thighs / nipples popping / hands on round hips / every touch embraces" ("This Year I Can't Complain," Irene Marcuse). It explores the taste of dampness and salt, the taste of caverns and crevices as the tongue plummets into a hidden cave. It honors juicy grapes rolled on the tip of the tongue, peaches firm in the hollow of the hand, blood-red ripe strawberries, a wheat field in seed, the fertile earth.

The third section, "Touching Fire," delves into the desire to merge with the life force. The thin, fine line distinguishing one body from another is approached sometimes leisurely, sometimes in a great rush of heat, until every nerve ending is blazing. Finally the line of separation dissolves. Everything surges into a union with infinity more beautiful and deep than we have ever imagined. Slowly, then, the boundaries reform. A leg is claimed here, an arm there. But the promise that this sense of oneness with the beloved and with life itself can happen again and again is intrinsic to all of the erotic. Gratefully we lick each other like cats, waiting.

The fourth section, "Restoring Spirit," joyously acclaims the body as the entranceway into the spiritual. This capacity of the body to merge with all of life and be transformed is perhaps what Lorde refers to when she writes of the "resource within us that lies in a deeply female and spiritual place . . . that creative energy empowered."

Through allowing ourselves to channel love, sensuality, and the force of life itself, we not only open ourselves to the healing of our individual wounds; we also begin to heal all of life. The body is sacred, blessed with skin, fingers delicately tracing lines of lips and eyes, lines of thighs etched in starlight, blessed with the long valley of the back, buttocks rounded like hills, the clitoris waiting to open in its pearly cave. The body, clothed in bone and sweet flesh, is a mirror of the spirit soaring through us and in us all.

When eros freely flows through us, this longing for life does not confine itself to the boundaries of our bodies but floods over sterile plains and renews broader forms of life. This kind of empowerment, when the life force in one's self is in harmony with the life force of the universe, is essential if our existence on this earth is to continue. For can we love and therefore honor, protect, and nourish life in any and all of its forms unless we have known the completion of desire within ourselves, loved our bodies, loved another, and been so loved?

The erotic in women's lives is thus an essential and powerful force. A primary purpose of this anthology is to convey the empowerment of living freely from one's erotic center: "As a child, my spirit was as indomitable as the wavy mass of hair on my head. Despite my mother's and hairdresser's considerable efforts to manage it, it has to this day remained untamed. The erotic for me is just this: this instinct toward passion that stubbornly defies all that threatens to subdue it. When my erotic self is intact, I am aroused by all that touches me and as I reach out, all that I touch resonates with the power of desire" (Deborah Abbott).

In order to begin living freely from our centers, women must be allowed to acknowledge and honor their eroticism. For centuries, while men were allowed and even encouraged to "sow their wild oats," women were not to give the slightest indication that they were sexual beings. The poet Susan Lysik alluded to this suppression when she wrote us: "Nice people don't talk about these things. I want to talk about being proud to be included in this book and being mortified that someone will tell my mother . . . I can't even name the parts of the body aloud without stammering."

Why must "nice" women be demure? If they are not, we

have been told, the very essence of life lived in harmony
with the cosmos is threatened. According to a prevalent
interpretation of the Adam and Eve myth, when Eve
"tempted" Adam, he ate of her forbidden fruit and thereby
brought Paradise crashing down around them. The splen-
dors of union with all of creation ended. Pain, grueling
work, and exile would be humanity's lot evermore—all because of Eve.

This interpretation suggests that a man is a very weak
creature having almost no will and that a woman is a powerful temptress. Thus a woman must assume responsibility both
for herself and any male unlucky enough to come under
her spell. In turn she must be dominated by men to keep
her from destroying life itself. In reality the reason she
must be dominated is that she is so greatly feared.

Underneath this fear may lie the question: If I surrender
to the lush, soft embrace of a woman or to the engulfing
passion of the Earth Mother/Life Force with all of my trust
and vulnerability, will I lose my very Self? The answer is:
Not unless this is what I desperately want. However, if I
desire an act of empowerment, a merging with another or
with Life itself and then a release into my own intact Self,
this is what I will be blessed with.

If we as women cannot express our intrinsic, life-affirming
erotic natures, we will continue to be shamed for having our
very bodies and will be coerced into allowing men to own
and thereby control them. If, on the other hand, we acknowledge that yes, we are sexual, we certainly do have
breasts and vulvas and other exquisite parts, we love making love, loving men, loving women, loving ourselves, we
claim our bodies as our own. And in this there is great
rejoicing.

The erotic, however, is more than the sexual. It includes
taking responsibility for our own lives: finding or creating
satisfying work, finding joy, allowing sorrow, allowing all
our feelings, choosing whether or not to act on those feelings, rejoicing in our bodies through running or giving
birth or making love or walking through clear light, opening our hearts, digging in the earth, planting.

We must not be deprived of this aspect of our eroticism
by waiting for Prince or Princess Charming to rescue us—
from our parents, from childhood pain, from a Self that we
cannot look at without despair. How many "erotic" novels,
plays, and movies have been based on a woman being
consumed/possessed/saved by another?

A woman deeply in touch with her own eroticism and acting out of this place is able to choose to join with another—or not. She does not allow herself to become obsessed with another. If she does become obsessed, she seeks healing for herself. She may *want* to be with a lover. She does not *need* to be with a lover.

If, however, the erotic in women is betrayed, as it is in pornography, women are left wounded and powerless. In essence this betrayal and that of child sexual abuse are the same. "Though child molestation is ostensibly condemned, it is in actuality sanctioned by our institutions, by movies, magazines, advertising, even art and literature. All of these confuse adult women with children; vulnerability with sexual invitation; masculinity with aggression; yes with no; women with their genitals; and both women and children with property owned by men."*

In both forms of abuse the integrity of the child or woman is violated. The child is no longer a vulnerable human being whom we as adults must cherish and protect; he or she is an object adults can use in whatever way they want. In like manner the women/objects in pornography are no longer whole, equal human beings, manifestations of the spirit made flesh. They are "tits," "cunts," and "holes."

In what is referred to as "soft porn," women are often portrayed as willing, ready, and powerless. Their mouths are open, the expressions on their faces suggest that they are on the verge of orgasm, and their bodies are often falling out of bits of clothing in various stages of disarray. They cannot wait, it seems, to be "banged" or "screwed" or "made" or "balled" or "laid" or "mounted." The violence in these acts is implicit.

In hardcore pornography, contempt for women and the desire to violate them is blatant. While the erotic writings in this anthology celebrate all that is vital, pornography celebrates a series of deaths as it robs women of the wholeness implicit in their connection with all of life.

To illustrate the difference between eros and "porn," I have chosen two photographs taken by two different photographers. In the first photograph (Edward Weston's "Nude, 1924") a nude woman is lying on her back, light forming a deep shadow along her left side so that there appear to

*Ellen Bass and Louise Thornton, editors. I Never Told Anyone: Writings by Women Survivors of Child Sexual Abuse. New York: Harper and Row, 1983.

be two women, one dark and abstract, shaped like a figure in a painting by Modigliani, and the other graced with light and almost floating above the dark shadow.

As I gaze at the photograph, my eyes travel along the woman's right leg crossed over her left leg, move to her breasts, rounded and arching above her rib cage, and then travel upward with the lines of the blanket stretching to the top of the photograph. From here my eyes move back down over her body suspended on the blanket and return again to the dark triangle stretching up from between her thighs. And here the journey begins again.

Thus as I look at the photograph my eye moves up, back down and around until I feel complete. This woman is whole, and I, who gaze at her and participate in her completeness, am also whole.

In the second photograph, taken by Clive McClean and featured in the April 1985 issue of *Hustler* magazine, a nude woman is lying on a bed, her legs raised high and spread as far apart as possible, her vulva open wide. A torn white blanket is wrapped around her shoulders and back and then gathered under her buttocks, which are positioned only a few inches from the camera's lens.

The woman's head is turned to one side. She seems to be in pain, her forehead creased by a furrow, mouth open, eyes closed. She cups her breasts with long, polished nails.

Because of the angle of the camera, my eyes are drawn immediately to the open lips of her vulva. My gaze travels briefly to the top of the photograph to see who belongs to this crotch. Then my eyes move down across the sharp fingernails beneath her breasts and look once more at the exposed, open lips.

The feelings I have at this point are discomfort and alienation. The pose is unnatural; after a short while it would be painful to hold the legs so far apart. Since the photographer focused on the vulva to such an extent that my eyes have almost nowhere else to go, I am distanced from this woman as a whole being. "I present this crotch," McClean seems to be saying, "but pay no attention to the woman who owns it as she is as inconsequential as the life of a trapped animal caught for her fur." In contrast, Weston seems to say: "I present this woman who is beautiful and whole."

Ann Simonton, the coordinator of an organization called Media Watch, which is concerned with how media images contribute to violence against women and children, articulates well the connection between pornography and powerlessness: "I am still discovering the infinite layers that reveal themselves to me concerning what porn images do and have done to my sexuality as a woman. Pornography still cuts me to the bone. I've shown thousands of students images of women sprawled on hamburger buns with ketchup dripping over their spread legs, women having their nipples torn off with pliers, women like baked turkey on a platter— their legs trussed up for serving . . . If I look intently at the slides my objectivity and voice evaporate. I am always amazed and horrified that such images cause amusement, entertainment, and arousal for men."*

The pornography she speaks of not only robs women of their wholeness; it carries powerlessness to its final end— the death of our sexuality, the death of our very being. Gloria Steinem says it more succinctly: "Erotoica is about sexuality, but pornography is about power and sex-as-weapon."**·We must not only rage against these murderous deaths. We must begin to redefine sexuality. Implicit in this definition is the belief that women shall always by regarded as subjects and treated as whole. So we begin by honoring sensuality: juices and tastes and tongues, bodies separate or joined. And we continue this definition by insisting that in any sexual encounter women freely act out of their intact erotic centers.

*A second memory: I am nine years old. My younger brother and sister and I are visiting my aunt and uncle's farm. In the barn we discover a loft filled with loose hay. For a long while we take turns swinging out over the hay on a rope and then letting go, falling into the alfalfa fragrant with sweetness and summer. Then my brother suggests that we play a secret game. It is an important game he tells us, because playing it will bring us children when we are grown. The more times we play it the more children we will have.*

*I become very curious. When our mother suddenly disappeared one day and came back a week later with a baby, she told us that when she decided she wanted another baby she told the doctor, who brought it to the hospital in his black bag. Perhaps there was some magical connection between a game you must play as a child and the babies waiting some where in doctors' black bags. My brother,*

---

*A. Simonton. "Pornography and Powerlessness." *Matrix*, July 1985: 4–5.
**Gloria Steinem. "Erotic and Pornographic: A Clear and Present Difference," in *Take Back the Night*. Wm. Morrow and Co., 1980.

*I decide, must know about these things because he roams the town while I stay home.*

*In the stillness of the loft on that summer afternoon I take down my underpants and lie on the hay. My little sister does the same. First my brother briefly touches my labia with his penis, then my sister's and then mine again. It seems like a silly game. Mostly it tickles. Then we jump up and run across the road to explore an old, abandoned schoolhouse. Here I decide that I want three children, so I ask my brother if we can do the touching again, and we do.*

*The next day my sister and I are playing in our yard, and she suddenly runs into the house. Terror surges through me. I know she is going to tell our mother about the game. Slowly I open the kitchen screen door and look into my mother's horribly contorted face. "I can't believe you did this!" she shouts. "And you had to drag your innocent little sister into it, too!" Then her voice becomes low and despairing and she looks away from me. "You were always my good little girl."*

*I want her to shout again or swat me—anything. Instead she picks up the baby and walks away. The perfect child I once was has turned into a nasty little girl. The adoring mother I once had is gone. I am lost.*

At this moment my unconscious made a number of decisions that would profoundly affect me for the next thirty years. The first decision was to split my body, which was "bad," from my mind, which was "good." I would live in my mind only. Second, if I did experience sensation I would quickly numb out any feelings and thereby protect myself from the "badness" of my body. The third decision was that I would never again ask for anything pleasurable.

Because these decisions were unconscious, their effects determined every action I took or failed to take. I spent the rest of my childhood isolated and excruciatingly lonely. I tried to be "good" to win approval and thereby love from my mother. When I was approached by a boy I froze. Although I longed for a boy's "love," it was nurturing I wanted, my mother now cold and distant. As I approached adulthood, the desire to be sexually intimate overwhelmed and terrified me, and I was often overcome with wrenching bouts of confusion and grief.

At the age of twenty-two I surrendered my virginity to my husband on our wedding night with an enormous sigh of relief. I enjoyed our sexuality! My erotic self was still alive after all. However, the internal, unconscious battle continued. I could not initiate lovemaking because the one time I did, my husband told me, "We shouldn't do it too much." This experience confirmed my belief that I could allow myself only a minimum amount of sexual pleasure.

All of these unresolved conflicts coupled with other problems in the marriage made me retreat even further into numbness. Heart pounding with terror, I would awake in the night unable to feel any sensation in my body. My God, I'm dying! I thought as I used the momentum of my body weight to throw myself out of bed and then pounded feeling back into my arms and legs. And I was.

Gathering up more courage than I thought I had, I took the advice of a friend to whom I shall be forever grateful and began seeing a therapist. This was at the age of forty. When I told my therapist about the sexual touching in the barn (I could barely get the words out, I was so ashamed) she did not think I was "bad." Instead she encouraged me to rage against my mother for her abandonment of me. After a long while I was able to do this and in the process of screaming and wailing I began to feel again.

Eventually I came to see my mother through the perspective of a wide cultural repression and violation of women's bodies. She simply repeated to me what had been said to her. I forgave my mother. After further work I forgave myself. Now I am coming to love the child who dared claim her body as her own that summer afternoon in the barn and who is beginning to delight once more in her sensual self.

I remember one afternoon in the bath perhaps five years ago. As I lay in the tub and let the water from the shower head stream against my clitoris, the beginning of an orgasm trembled in my body. It built and then swept through me with an intensity I had never known, and I screamed and shouted with ecstatic abandon. When I was again quiet, I thought: this is a gift. Life has given me this capacity for intense pleasure. I do not have to earn it or be ashamed of it or deny it. I am blessed and whole.

The battle between my life-affirming, erotic self and my judgmental, life-suppressing self was not won once and for all that afternoon. But it was a beginning, and it is in the sensual realm that I continue to heal.

Eros, then, is a gift given in the trust that it will be used to enhance life, that we can in turn trust this vulnerability to each other, that even if this trust is violated we are capable of renewal. For it is life that desires us, longs for us, whole.

# Rousing the Waters

# Alice Munro

# Baptizing

The unreality, long-drawn-out embarrassment, and tedium of the evening vanished in the cab of the truck, in the smell of its old split seats, and poultry feed, the sight of Garnet's rolled-up sleeves and bare forearms, of his hands, loose and alert on the wheel. Black rain on the closed windows sheltered us. Or if the rain was over we would roll down the windows and feel the rank soft air near the invisible river, smell mint crushed under the truck wheels, where we pulled off the road to park. We nosed deep into the bushes, which scratched against the hood. The truck stopped with a last little bump that seemed a signal of achievement, permission, its lights, cutting weakly into the density of night, went out, and Garnet turned to me always with the same sigh, the same veiled and serious look, and we would cross over, going into a country where there was perfect security, no move that would not bring delight; disappointment was not possible. Only when I was sick, with a fever, had I ever before had such a floating feeling, feeling of being languid and protected and at the same time possessing unlimited power. We were still in the approaches to sex, circling, backtracking, hesitating, not because we were afraid or because we had set any sort of prohibition on "going too far" (such explicitness, in that country, and with Garnet, was next to unthinkable) but because we felt an obligation as in the game of our hands on the back of the chair, not to hurry, to make shy, formal, temporary retreats in the face of so much pleasure. That very word, *pleasure*, had changed for me; I used to think it a mild sort of word, indicating a rather low-key self-indulgence; now it seemed explosive, the two vowels in the first syllable spurting up like fireworks, ending on the plateau of the last syllable, its dreamy purr.

15

I would go home from these sessions by the river and not be able to sleep sometimes till dawn, not because of unrelieved tension, as might be expected, but because I had to review, could not let go of, those great gifts I had received, gorgeous bonuses—lips on the wrists, the inside of the elbow, the shoulders, the breasts, hands on the belly, the thighs, between the legs. Gifts. Various kisses, tongue touchings, suppliant and grateful noises. Audacity and revelation. The mouth closed frankly around the nipple seemed to make an avowal of innocence, defenselessness, not because it imitated a baby's but because it was not afraid of absurdity. Sex seemed to me all surrender—not the woman's to the man but the person's to the body, an act of pure faith, freedom in humility. I would lie washed in these implications, discoveries, like somebody suspended in clear and warm and irresistibly moving water, all night.

# Doreen Stock

# Twilight

It begins under the wing of an airplane.

The air navy blue and full of warm mist.

The one who was, to you, when you were the child, the sweetest love, the unfailing one, the beacon, this one stands there.

Words are not allowed.

The two of you wait there, under the wing of the plane. One is to leave, of course, one is to stay. It was all arranged long before you were born. Began to rise and flourish slowly in the milky grass, in the green arrows swirling round a stem. You learned to stand and then to walk, toward someone, always toward someone, traveling the blue lines to their eyes.

And the dandelions were all over the hill, in the grass, dandelions, the flowers.

And in your first mouthful of kiss, there, all along as you tumbled in hay, in snow, lips, teeth, little bump of sex under you, over you.

"Oh earth," your body learned to say, first in one, then another, "oh earth!"

"You know what, honey?" said my first love over the telephone wire at thirteen.

"What, honey?"

"Whenever I want to talk to her, to my grandma, I choose a star, a special star, and talk, just to her."

And one by one the dandelions torn up.

The neighbors priding themselves on their front lawn. A tool to uproot each one, each flower removed, the tool pushed by hand down under the root. Breaking sound as the roothairs decide. "I'm staying," they say and snap under the surface.

The dandelions, lying in heaps on the grass. Late afternoon. Sound of withering. Itchy sweet-sour smell. Piling

17

them up finally in the grocery carton. To mingle, damp, with the cardboard.

All night brother and sister whispering in our beds. Secret codes we had then. And outside, the holes in the green. How does the grass grow so quietly in the night? Over the holes. So when you get up in the morning and look outside the little holes have almost closed their eyes. And in the box everything has sunk down.

Another night. Maybe you cry out in your sleep. A tear under an eyelash. And that is the grass. The dew under it.

It was all being arranged then. The miraculous presences to infect you. Juices that would splash and sing. Stems like bubblegum and rubber. How to make crowns. How to laugh and put them in each other's hair. Blue-and-white checked shirt. Spring, oh spring. Walking in dandelions barefoot their milk streaking your ankles, running, running, always toward someone.

"Star light, star bright, first star I see tonight. Wish I may, wish I might, have the wish I wish tonight."

Grandma, when I was little and couldn't find you in the night. Or took the bus to meet you and got lost downtown. You smiled, told me, "You have a mouth. You speak English. There's no reason, honey, for you ever to be lost."

It begins under the wing of an airplane. The air navy blue and full of warm mist.

Words are not allowed.

You turn toward each other and the long kiss, the long pull, the arms around you toward the stars, begins.

# Janet Aalfs

# The Secret

**1.**

I am a life-buoy and you are a small, slippery sea-creature, clinging to my neck, my shoulders, not yet at home. I carry you to the shallows and we wade, ankle-deep, searching for crabs. A small one, faded, floats belly-up near a rock, its claws slack. Reaching for it, you stumble and I grab you, like I might a small child. I am ten Augusts old and you are eight. No one wonders why I hold you like this. They are all thinking—the mothers and fathers, the sisters and brothers, the friends—that I will grow up to be a good mother. And you, the innocent one, play and fall down and get up again, sure that someone will be there to catch you. So I do.

**2.**

Your mother whispers to me that you still believe in Santa Claus. I listen as you tell me excitedly about the things Santa will stuff down the chimney into your living room. Nodding my head, I congratulate you on your good fortune. My brother, who is your age, does not spoil your joy either. He and I look at each other and for a moment, believe that it is you who know the truth—your hopeful eyes, your shiny dark hair, your skipping the lines on the sidewalk to make the day of surprises come sooner. I hide this secret from you. To protect you, I believe.

**3.**

Water spreads fanlike, rainbows weaving in and out between thin lines of spray. Back and forth the sprinkler

19

arches, falling first to one side, then growing, curling up
and out like a fern, before cresting and rolling, watering the
lawn. We run beneath this canopy, daring each other to
dash before the fan topples and covers us with cold fingers.
Your hair, wet and sleek; the drops on your olive skin, tiny
magnifying glasses reflecting the sun. You are radiant. Back
and forth our footsteps, the sprinkler. Puddles on the brick
patio, puddles in the grass turning to mud. Sure-footed,
you do not care that the mud splashes up your legs, splat-
ters your shorts. Laughing, I watch you slip and slide, never
falling. Chasing you, I am the wind pushing you forward.
*Careful*, I hear your mother calling. I hear it on the wind
and in the splashing water. I hear it in my brain and in my
heart. *Careful*, the suck of mud. *Careful*, the soft thud of our
feet. *Careful*, the sharp smack of your head as you hit the
unyielding brick. I scream. Too late.

Your mother holds the icepack firmly against your forehead with one hand. With the other, she presses a once-
white handkerchief beneath your nose, plugging your nostrils
from which ooze large clots of dark red blood and tissue. I
sit on the hassock next to the couch where you lie so still,
barely breathing. It is dark in your living room, even at the
bright of noon, and cool, like water. But you are no longer
laughing. I cannot stop your falling, or your blood, or your
tears.

After the bleeding subsides, I watch you climb into the
car next to your mother. Later I call and you tell me in a
nasal voice that you've been to the doctor. *My nose*, you say.
*They had to cauterize it again.* You describe how they put a
burning rod inside your nostrils to seal the damaged tissue.
*But it might not work.* Lying on your back with an icepack on
your forehead, you watch baseball on TV in the dark living
room. The water in your yard keeps falling.

Down the street at my house, the slate steps are hard and
cold and I sit here, waiting. I cannot say what I am waiting
for—maybe for you to feel better and come outside with
me. But you do not appear.


**4.**


We are ankle-deep in mud, thigh-deep in water. Searching the river bottom for quahogs; stepping lightly we feel
with our toes, then reach with our hands, arms shoulder-
deep in water to retrieve the hard white shells. The rowboat

bobs on the small wind-whipped waves. I hold the rope and pull the boat over to drop another bucketful of quahogs into the turquoise Fiberglas hull. A tern screams at us and dives toward our heads, swooping back up to ride the wind as we duck, shielding our skulls with one free arm. They never attack, only threaten. But that does not stop us from cowering.

Back at the cottage, your mother drops our catch into a large pot of boiling water as we watch. She puts the lid on and the steam hisses out, a light cloud above the stove, misting the window. Your grandfather sits outside in a lawn chair, jackknife in hand, slitting the muscle and eating the sea-creatures raw. I am sickened and cannot watch. When the ones in the pot have opened, your mother takes them off the flame and pours out the milky liquid. A layer of mud sits at the bottom of the pot. We each pick a shellfish carefully from the pile and pry it all the way open. Inside, the flesh is still soft and warm, as if it were alive; around the belly, a thin line of mud that I trace with the tip of my index finger. It tastes like salt, like rock, like a dark ocean secret. *Open me*, I whisper into my hand.

**5.**

I am big for my age. You are small. I pretend you are my daughter. I hold you in my arms, in the water, and feel your smooth forehead against my neck. I press your body into mine and you shiver; I hold you closer. The waves rock us back and forth and you cling—I, to my neck in water; you unable to touch the bottom with your toes. We stay this way until your mother calls us back to shore. I let you down gently in shallow water, and you run, hair flying, thin legs churning the water, spray flying up like a shield in front of you as you push your feet through the waves. Your mother shakes her head and wishes you were more like me. But she would not want to know the truth. Why I hold you so close in the water; how your skin feels smooth and warm against mine; how when I am in bed at night, I wrap my arms tight around myself and pretend you are there. Like magic. I am touching myself, opening a shell. I rub my fingertip slowly around the edges, then dip into folds of flesh, alive and pulsing, warm and wet. *I swear to you that no one will ever find out. I promise, I will not tell.*

## Cerridwen Fallingstar

# Excerpt from The Heart of the Fire

*The Heart of the Fire* is an historical novel on witchcraft set in sixteenth century Scotland. The narrator is Fiona McNair, a peasant girl who is academically ignorant but apprenticed to the old shamanic traditions of magic and nature worship.

Like every loss of innocence, it started innocently enough. We were twelve, brash hooligans wild as lynx or lark or the unpredictable spring storms. We were still not above stealing the horseshoes over someone's barn or tying elf-locks in their horses' manes and tails. We could be thoughtful, leaving bunches of flowers on people's doorsteps. On the other hand, we were just as likely to leave a basket of snails. Early April, the ground already thawing. Annie's cat had just had kittens.

Up in the loft, tickling each other into hysteria rolling off the blanket into the hay, yellow prickles in our hair. "Ow! Stop yer silliness!" giggles snickers snorts horsy smells in our noses. "You be the kitten an' I'll be Tawny," you say. "If yer the mumcat where are yer teats?" Russet kitten I become, pawing through your clothes in search of milk. I find your slight breast and latch on. Your turn to cry out and cuff me. "Ow, damn kitten. I think yer father was a robber lynx! Coory doon bairn tis time for yer bath." I make no protest as she undresses me. We've slept and played naked together often, to both our mothers' distress. "Gypsy brat!" her mother would screech at her when Annie palmed the bannocks or rifled her purse, or cut up her clothes into costumes no decent person would wear. Everyone expected Annie to be bad since her father was a wicked thieving gypsy. Bad she was.

But what a sweet tongue she had. Not rough like Tawny's, so smooth and warm. My skin rumpled into goose-prickles along the paths her tongue left wet to the air. But who would complain? This shivering was different from any I'd ever known, quivering in such a strange way that even as my skin prickled I got warmer and warmer. The between-my-legs part felt the most shivery of all. As she moved from my breast to my ribs across my belly I knew that I wanted her to put her mouth there. Instead she went down my leg oh under the knees nipping my toes, teeth sharp as a cat's then licking my thighs oh my belly my flat nipples or her tongue sharp on my nipples the between-my-legs part is burning aching hot but it feels good how can anything that sharp feel good? Under my arms and down my arms. "Yer s'pose to purr," she says. I have been holding my breath obediently I purr between short gasps wanting her to touch between my legs more than ever and wondering at my wish. She turns me over licking and biting along my shoulders and neck purring or growling at me occasionally is this still a game? I cannot bear it and want her to never stop, her licking at the lower curve of my ass I biting my lip and holding my breath again feeling like I'm about to turn into air or steam. Turning over, "Annie . . ." She shushes me kissing my thighs again she is kissing not licking then she is cautiously pushing my trembling thighs apart looking up into my eyes. "D'ye want to play?" her eyes question see the answer in mine then her tongue touching me and I moan she stops. "Did that hurt?" "No," I whisper "please . . ." her tongue touching me again caressing that wrinkle of flesh at the center of my cleft. It does hurt and I feel some deep opening, some emptiness that never felt empty before. Then something happens and I dissolve in wetness tears flowing out of my eyes. I come back to myself clutching her shoulders she lying on top of me propped up on her forearms, looking searchingly into my damp gaze, "Are ye alreet?" I'm not sure what I am but I nod and smile. "Good." Annie huffs down beside me. "Then tis my turn to be the kitten and ye be the mumcat."

I soon discovered that I could make Annie melt like she had made me. Her body got very tense as I licked her and for awhile I thought she was wroth with me 'cause when I reminded her to keep purrin' she said "Not now!" in a harsh voice. But then she grabbed my hair and pressed my face deeper into her cleft and cried out I tasted smoke salt flowers and again dissolved.

Later we kissed and solemnly swore to keep our new knowledge a secret. But Annie and I did not know the

meaning of the word discretion. Oh, we did not actually talk
to anyone about it, and at first probably no one suspected.
But as we grew older other villagers began to narrow their
eyes at us running down the street holding hands or saun-
tering in the smithy or at the Inn with our arms around
each other.

One day at the smithy watching John Herrick at his trade.
Sean, the Laird's son, watching wistfully the smith's skill for
he longed to make things with his hands. Several other
village men lounging near the forge drinking whiskey for
comfort against the cold winds. Annie and I with our cloaks
around each other clinging together for warmth the smoky
smell of her hair in my nostrils. The men called for us to
come sit in their laps share their whiskey and get warm.
Their laughter is hearty the lewdness of their interest obvious. I'm no insulted but I'm no tempted neither. Annie
feels too good to move. "We're fine as we are," I call back.
"Yer too old tae be clinging tae each other like snooty-nosed
bairns," one joshes. "An too smart tae be clinging tae the likes
of you," retorts Annie, kissing me full on the mouth in
front of them. We toss our hair like wild horses and canter
off through the snow, laughing at the looks on their faces.
But while I laugh I feel a cold hard knot in my middle, a
fear that someday these men will remember us playing
them for fools, and pay us back for it.

## Zora Neale Hurston

# Excerpt from Their Eyes Were Watching God

It was a spring afternoon in West Florida. Janie had spent most of the day under a blossoming pear tree in the backyard. She had been spending every minute that she could steal from her chores under that tree for the last three days. That was to say, ever since the first tiny bloom had opened. It had called her to come and gaze on a mystery. From barren brown stems to glistening leaf-buds; from the leaf-buds to snowy virginity of bloom. It stirred her tremendously. How? Why? It was like a flute song forgotten in another existence and remembered again. What? How? Why? This singing she heard that had nothing to do with her ears. The rose of the world was breathing out smell. It followed her through all her waking moments and caressed her in her sleep. It connected itself with other vaguely felt matters that had struck her outside observation and buried themselves in her flesh. Now they emerged and quested about her consciousness.

She was stretched on her back beneath the pear tree soaking in the alto chant of the visiting bees, the gold of the sun and the panting breath of the breeze when the inaudible voice of it all came to her. She saw a dust-bearing bee sink into the sanctum of a bloom; the thousand sister-calyxes arch to meet the love embrace and the ecstatic shiver of the tree from root to tiniest branch creaming in every blossom and frothing with delight. So this was a marriage! She had been summoned to behold a revelation. Then Janie felt a pain remorseless sweet that left her limp and languid.

After a while she got up from where she was and went over the little garden field entire. She was seeking confirmation of the voice and vision, and everywhere she found and acknowledged answers. A personal answer for all other creations except herself. She felt an answer seeking her, but where? When? How? She found herself at the kitchen door and stumbled inside. In the air of the room were flies tumbling and singing, marrying and giving in marriage. When she reached the narrow hallway she was reminded that her grandmother was home with a sick headache. She was lying across the bed asleep so Janie tipped on out of the front door. Oh to be a pear tree—*any* tree in bloom! With kissing bees singing of the beginning of the world! She was sixteen. She had glossy leaves and bursting buds and she wanted to struggle with life but it seemed to elude her. Where were the singing bees for her? Nothing on the place nor in her grandma's house answered her. She searched as much of the world as she could from the top of the front steps and then went on down to the front gate and leaned over to gaze up and down the road. Looking, waiting, breathing short with impatience. Waiting for the world to be made.

Through pollinated air she saw a glorious being coming up the road. In her former blindness she had known him as shiftless Johnny Taylor, tall and lean. That was before the golden dust of pollen had beglamored his rags and her eyes.

In the last stages of Nanny's sleep, she dreamed of voices. Voices far-off but persistent, and gradually coming nearer. Janie's voice. Janie talking in whispery snatches with a male voice she couldn't quite place. That brought her wide awake. She bolted upright and peered out of the window and saw Johnny Taylor lacerating her Janie with a kiss.

"Janie!"

The old woman's voice was so lacking in command and reproof, so full of crumbling dissolution—that Janie half believed that Nanny had not seen her. So she extended herself outside of her dream and went inside of the house. That was the end of her childhood.

# Amber Coverdale Sumrall

## Paper Boy

*for Peter Osbaldeston*

Every Thursday afternoon, I wait by the window, for Peter to ride by our house. Once a week he delivers the local paper on a bicycle he outgrew two years ago. Peter is a refugee from Budapest; his family fled Hungary when the Communists took over.

Peter has a faint mustache like a shadow, and long, chestnut brown hair that falls over his face on one side. All the other eighth-grade boys have crewcuts. Peter tosses his hair back from his eyes like a horse shaking its mane.

I want to ride him.

I want him to ride me, like my brother does sometimes. I'll lie on the floor and Patrick will sit on me and bounce up and down. We pretend we're playing horse and cowboy.

I want Peter to ride me like this.

My girlfriends think Peter is homely. Homely and weird. I don't tell them how much I want him to touch me. They'd think I was weirder than he is. Peter plays the violin and is a straight-A student. The nuns say he's a genius. He doesn't have any friends and keeps to himself.

Peter has six brothers and sisters. He helps support his family by delivering papers. They live in a run-down, two-bedroom house near my friend Lynn. I ride my bike over to her house every chance I get, in hopes of seeing Peter, but he's never outside. I know he babysits the neighbor kids. That's one of the reasons everyone thinks he's so weird. Especially the boys; they call him a sissy.

I feel like I'm being pulled in half whenever I'm around him. At school I can't speak to him; my words come out like some foreign language or not at all. I have a hard time breathing if he notices me. I stare at the back of his head so hard sometimes, that I think we will both go up in flames, become tongues of fire like the Holy Ghost.

I want to take his hand and lead him out to the tall grass

27

behind the playground. I want to unbutton my blouse and show him my new breasts. I want to feel the weight of his slender body holding me to the ground. I can't concentrate in class or do my homework anymore. I write his name over and over: inside my binder, my books, on the bottoms of my shoes.

I think I will die if I can't touch him.

For the last month I've come home early on Thursdays so I could be at the window when Peter rides by. I've spent the rest of the afternoon daydreaming (that's what Mother calls it) in my room. I move like I'm in a trance when she calls me to come set the table.

But today I'm home extra early. I didn't stop to buy ice cream or look at the new issue of *Seventeen* with Jeanie and Sheryl. I told them I had to do chores.

I change into my white shorts and apricot blouse. I unbutton the first two buttons, but my bra shows so I decide to take it off. It's probably a mortal sin, but who cares as long as Mother doesn't notice. I brush out my hair, tie it back into a ponytail, and wrap a satin ribbon around it. Mother is flabbergasted when I tell her I'm going to pick weeds in the front yard.

"Dressed like that?" she says. "If you stain those new shorts, young lady, I won't buy you another pair." She looks at me strangely. I slouch, sink my chest in, and hold my breath.

"I hope you aren't dressed up for Butch Willis's sake."

Butch is the creep across the street. He's three years older than me, the neighborhood bully. He likes to snap his long bullwhip in the street on Saturday mornings. It keeps the younger kids inside. He teases my brother every chance he gets. I hate him! Once I let all his birds out of their cage in his backyard after he made my brother cry.

"Oh Mother, *really*," I say. "I can't stand Butch Willis. He makes me puke."

She tells me to watch my language.

"Well, that's not the way he feels about you," she says. "Marge thinks he has quite a crush on you. He writes your name all over his bedroom walls."

"That's disgusting, Mother. He gives me the creeps." I shudder and leave the kitchen before she remembers my white shorts again.

In the bathroom I sneak her tube of Tangee and dab my lips until they are the same color as my blouse. I wish I was beautiful like Ann, the cheerleader two doors down. She's my age, but has big breasts and curved hips. She saw me crying last year after Mother made me cut my long hair. *Ann's* hair hangs down to her waist.

It's after four, so I grab a box and go sit on the front lawn with the trowel. Ten minutes later, Peter rides around the corner. I immediately begin to shake and wonder if I can act like I don't care about him. Suzi says that's what boys like best. It attracts them like flies she says.

I get up feeling dizzy and walk to the edge of the driveway, pretending to weed close to the curb. Peter throws a paper on the porch next door then, . . . oh my God, stops right in front of me.

"Oh . . . hi," I say, as nonchalantly as possible. He hands me our paper and smiles: a lingering, crooked smile that reaches deep down to my bones. I forget to breathe, hope I don't faint like Beatrice Moore does every Sunday at Mass. My carefully rehearsed words vanish like answers before a test and I blurt out, . . . "I want you."

My hands fly to my mouth. Peter's eyes twinkle. "You want me . . . to . . . ?" His eyes never leave my face.

"I want you . . . to . . . help me with my math," I say, praying he believes me.

"I'll even pay you. My mother says I need a tutor."

"I can't do that," he says gently. "I don't have time. I work or help out at home whenever I'm not in school."

"But this *will* be work."

I will drop to my knees in front of him, beg, wash his feet, do whatever he says. Anything!

He looks at me like he can see into my soul. Maybe he's a saint. That would explain why he affects me this way.

"No, I really can't help you," Peter says. "I'm sorry."

I feel unable to move, paralyzed by his rejection. How could he do this to me? It's not like he's the best looking or most popular boy in our class. Far from it!

I want to hurt him.

"Don't you ever *play*, Peter?" I taunt him, in my most sarcastic tone.

He shifts on his bike; his olive face darkens. Oh my God, I've hurt him. Oh God, please make him forgive me.

"I don't have time for play," he says. "I'm studying to be a classical musician." Peter looks at me, then suddenly reaches out and touches my face.

"I've got to go now." He pushes off from the curb.

I have so many feelings churning inside I don't know

what to do or say. It's all I can do just to stand here. I want
to run after him crying, "Peter, I love you. I'm sorry." But I
think somehow he knows.

I watch his legs pump up and down. The papers fly from
his hands. He turns and smiles again. Then disappears
from sight.

# Sharon Olds

# First Sex
*for J.*

I knew little, and what I knew
I did not believe—they had lied to me
so many times, so I just took it as it
came, his naked body on the sheet,
the tiny hairs curling on his legs like
fine, gold shells, his sex
harder and harder under my palm
and yet not hard as a rock his face cocked
back as if in terror, the sweat
jumping out of his pores like sudden
trails from the tiny snails when his knees
locked with little clicks and under my
hand he gathered and shook and the actual
flood like milk came out of his body, I
saw it glow on his belly, all they had
said and more, I rubbed it into my
hands like lotion, I signed on for the duration.

# Susan Lysik

# I Am Horny

I wish there were a nicer word
for this
walking
     on
       the
         edge

My flesh is so full
I expect the skin to burst,
gently at first
like the sweetest plum,
then ragged and gaping with neglect,
spoiled,
leaving only the hard kernel
to begin again the
cycle of ripeness and waiting

Now I rub my feet
back    and forth
back    and forth
between the flowered sheets
They are new
and I can count every thread

Back    and forth
I press my body full into the yielding mattress
The pressure soothes me
The muslin becomes a soft skin,
cool against my own

*Just last week I was finished with relationships,*
*celebrating the steadiness of my balance alone*
*This poem is not about*
*relationships*

32

\*     \*     \*

Yesterday it was the man who
came to insulate the attic
His lean tattooed body sparks my
sharp breath when our
shoulders brush in the doorway

We discuss fiberglass
while my fingers covet
the sweet arc of his jaw,
his thick black hair
   my hands
   his hair   He knows
his white smile can
blind a woman:   Hey
mama, hey
The easy walk, mama
the even teeth and quick familiarity, mama
weaken my knees

I'm not
your mama
        is
the correct response,
but I cannot
The truth of it is
that right then
with the light just so on his dark face
I could betray anything

The moment shimmers
He makes a joke
about coming back later
but he will not
This man could deal with a simple need
but mine is not that pure
   Even when I don't want anything at all
   I want more than that

And today,
today it will be someone in the grocery
by the cheese case perhaps
or the condiments
Tomorrow some arrogance on the beach
opaque against the full sun

*     *     *

Sooner or later
someone will pick it up
By that time it will be too late to resist
too late
to carry out the plan not to sleep with strangers

There will be the flashing together
and how am I to avoid taking it seriously
How am I
            to avoid taking it
                        at all

My body betrays my resolution
Liar, it says
liar
You'd turn over rocks when your blood runs this way

This poem is about wanting someone
to trace the line of my suntan
gently
over and over      gently
with one careful finger
until I fall asleep at last

> *This poem is*
> *about relationships*

# Adrienne Rich

## Re-Forming the Crystal

I am trying to imagine
how it feels to you
to want a woman

trying to hallucinate
desire
centered in a cock
focused like a burning-glass

desire without discrimination:
to want a woman like a fix

Desire: yes: the sudden knowledge, like coming out of flu,
that the body is sexual. Walking in the streets with that
knowledge. That evening in the plane from Pittsburgh,
fantasizing going to meet you. Walking through the airport
blazing with energy and joy. But knowing all along that you
were not the source of that energy and joy; you were a man,
a stranger, a name, a voice on the telephone, a friend; this
desire was mine, this energy my energy; it could be used a
hundred ways, and going to meet you could be one of
them.

Tonight is a different kind of night.
I sit in the car, racing the engine,
calculating the thinness of the ice.
In my head I am already threading the beltways
that rim this city,
all the roads that used to wander the country
having been lost.
Tonight I understand
my photo on the license is not me,
my

name on the marriage-contract was not mine.
If I remind you of my father's favorite daughter,
look again. The woman
I needed to call my mother
was silenced before I was born.

Tonight if the battery charges I want to take the car out on
sheet-ice; I want to understand my fear both of the masculine and of the accidents of nature. My desire for you is not
trival; I can compare it with the greatest of those accidents.
But the energy it draws on might lead to racing a cold
engine, cracking the frozen spiderweb, parachuting into the
field of a poem wired with danger, or to a trip through
gorges and canyons, into the cratered night of female memory, where delicately and with intense care the chieftainess
inscribes upon the ribs of the volcano the name of the one
she has chosen.

## Amber Coverdale Sumrall

# Womantides

My hair spreads like seaweed
  in the wake of your mouth.
We are clams in sea rhythm
  surrendering
    to the gentle clasp of teeth.

Your fingers are whispers
  tides high and low.
Your mouth traces secrets
  back to their source.

I want the swell of your hands
  beached deep inside me
    the slow lap of your tongue.

# Terry L. McMillan

# Touching

I suspected someone was there in that *very* same spot before me, but I didn't let the thought grow in my mind or rot there, till I saw her swinging on your side like a shoulder-strap purse early this morning. And this was after I had already let you touch me all over with your long brown hands and break down my resistance, so that you left me feeling like the earth had been pulled from under my feet.

First, I see your lean long legs coming toward me on that crooked gray sidewalk, the silver specks glaring in my eyes like dancing stars. But I was not blinded, even when you dragged them in that elegant, yet pompous kinda way of yours. And you watched me coming from at least a half a block away and those size 13s didn't seem to lift up off the cement as high as they did the other night when we walked down this *very* same street together.

I know it was me who called you up the other night to say hello, but it was *you* who invited me to come down and walk your dog with you. Sounded innocent enough to me, but all along I'm sure you knew that I wanted to finally find out how warm it was under your shirt, behind your zipper, and if your hands were as gentle and strong as they looked. I was really hoping we could skip the walk altogether 'cause I just wanted to fall down on you slowly and get to your insides. Walk the dog another time. But since you could've misconstrued my motives as being unladylike, I bounced on down the street to your apartment in my white jogging outfit, trying to look as alluring as I possibly could, but without looking too eager.

I even dabbed gold oil behind my ears, under each breast and on the tips of my elbows so as to lure you closer to me in case you couldn't make up your mind. The truth of the matter is that I was nervous because I knew that we weren't gonna just chitchat tonight like we'd done before. I went out of my way in five minutes flat to brush my teeth twice, put on fresh coats of red lipstick, wash under my arms, Q-tip my ears and navel ('cause I didn't know just how far you might want to go), and wash my most intimate areas and sprinkle a little jasmine oil there too.

Even though it was almost ninety degrees, we walked fifteen blocks and the dog didn't let go of anything. You didn't seem to mind or notice. You handed me the leash, and even though I can't stand to see a grown man with a little cutesy-wutesy dog, I wasn't hostile as I tugged at it as we continued to walk through the thick night air. For the most part, I like dogs.

When our feet dropped from the curb, and I jumped and screamed because a fallen leaf looked like a dead mouse, I let go of the leash and grabbed your hand. You squeezed it back, though you had to drag me to chase after your dog, who had taken off down the sidewalk, running up to the tree's bark and just panting. When we finally caught him, we were both out of breath. I regretted wearing that sweaty jogging suit.

"You scared of a little mouse?" you asked.

"Yes, they give me the heebie-jeebies. My stomach turns over and I want to jump on top of chairs and stuff just to get away from them."

Then you told me about the time you busted one on your kitchen counter eating your ravioli right out of the can and how you wounded it with a broomstick and then tried to flush it down the toilet, but it wouldn't flush. I laughed loud and hard, but I wanted to make you laugh, too.

So, I told you about the time I was on my way out of my house to take a sauna when I accidently saw a giant roach cavorting on my kitchen counter. I whacked it with my right hand just hard enough to cripple it. (I am scared of mice but I hate roaches.) I didn't want it to die immediately because I had just spent $9.95 on some Roach-Pruf which I had ordered through the newspaper and wanted to see if it *really* worked. So, I sprinkled about a quarter teaspoon on his head as he was about to struggle to find a crack or crevice somewhere. He kept on trying so I kept on sprinkling more Pruf on his antennae. After five minutes of this, he was getting on my nerves 'cause I still had my coat on, my purse and gym bag thrown over my shoulders, and since my kitchen was designed strictly with dwarfs and children in mind, I was burning up. It was then that I decided to burn him up too. First I lit myself a cigarette, and with the same match, burned off his antennae but the sucker still kept trying to get to one corner of the counter. I got real mad because my Pruf was obviously not working and I just went ahead and burnt him up quickly and totally for not dying the way he was supposed to.

You thought this was terribly funny and cracked up. I liked hearing you laugh, but I didn't know if you thought this was indicative of my personality: torture and murder and everything.

We continued to walk a few more blocks, making small talk and the dog contined running up to tree trunks, kicking up his little white legs and finally squirting out wetness, but that was about it.

By this time, I was sweating and picturing your head nestled between my breasts. I like feeling a man's head there, and it had been so long since any man even made me feel like dreaming out loud, that I didn't even hear you when you asked me if I liked the Temptations and had I ever been to a puppet show. I didn't understand the connection until we walked inside your apartment.

Today though, you watched me come toward you like this was a tug-of-war, but the rope was invisible. The gravity was so dense that it pulled us face to face and when I finally reached you I could smell your breath at the end of the rope. You were uneasy, and sorta turned in a half-turn toward me as I brushed past both of you. You loosely smiled back at me, squinting behind those tinted glasses, and I smiled back at both of you 'cause I don't have a grudge with this girl; wasn't *her* who I spent the night with.

"What are *you* doing up so early?" you asked. I didn't really think it was any of your business since you didn't call last night to see how late I was up. Besides, it was almost ten o'clock in the morning.

"I've already had my coffee, done my laundry, and now I'm trying to get to the plant store to buy some dirt so I can transplant my fern and rubber tree before the block party this afternoon."

'Oh, I'm sorry, Marie, this is Carolyn," you said, waving your hands between us like a magician.

We both nodded like ladies, fully understanding your uneasiness.

"Why don't you have the Chinese people do your laundry?" you asked.

"Because I like to know that my clothes are clean; I like to fold them up nice and neat like I want them. And besides, I like to put things together that belong together."

You just nodded your head like a fool. For a moment you looked puzzled, like someone had dropped you off in the middle of nowhere. You didn't seem to mind either that the girl was standing there watching your poise alter and sway. Me neither. But I had to move away from you 'cause I could really smell your body scent now and it was starting to stick to my skin, gravitating around me, until it got all up into my nostrils and then hit my brain, swelled up my whole head right there on the spot. This was embarrassing, so I tried to play it off by pulling my scarlet scarf down closer toward my eyebrows. But you already knew what had happened.

I make my feet move away from you as if I am trying to catch a bus I see approaching. I take my hands and wipe away the burnt-red lipstick from my mouth and cheeks at the mere thought of letting you press yours against them. Was trying to forget how handsome you were altogether. Fine. Too fine. Didn't listen to my mama. "Never look at a man that's prettier than you, 'cause he's gonna act that way." I was trying to think about dirt. The leaves of my plants. But I never have been attracted to pretty men, I thought, trying to miss the cracks in the sidewalk after stubbing my toe. You were different. Spoke correct English. Made puppets move and talk. Wrote your own grant proposals. Drank herbal tea and didn't smoke cigarettes. You crossed your legs and arms when you talked, and leaned your wide shoulders back in your chair so your behind slid to the edge. Made me think you thought about the words before letting them roll off your tongue. I admired you for contemplating things before you made them happen.

You yelled at me after I was almost halfway down the block. "Are you selling anything at the block party?"

I had already told you the other day I was making zucchini cake, but I repeated it again. "Zucchini cake!" and waved good-bye, trying to keep that stupid grin on my face though I know you wouldn't have been able to see my expression from a distance.

I liked the attention you were giving me in spite of the girl. I thought it meant something. I was even hoping as I trucked into the plant store and got stuck by a cactus that you would call me later on to explain that she was just a friend or your cousin or your sister. I was hoping that you would tell me that your back hurt or something so I could come down with my almond oil and rub it for you. Beat it, dig my fingertips into your shoulder blades and the canals along your spine until you gave in. Or maybe you would tell me you broke your glasses and couldn't see. I would come down and read out loud to you: comic books or the Bible.

Now, I'm out here on this sidewalk with a bag of black dirt in my hands in the heat walking past your house, forcing myself not to stare up at those dingy white shutters of yours so I twist my neck in the opposite direction, looking ridiculous and completely conspicuous. I thought for sure I was gonna be your one-and-only-down-the-street sweetheart, 'cause I carried myself like a lady, not like some dog in heat.

I really had no intention of transplanting anything today. I just told you that because it sounded clean. I was more concerned about whether this girl touched you last night the way I had. Probably not, because only I can touch you the way I touch you. But as you were standing there on that sidewalk, I kept seeing still shots of us flashing across my eyes: twisting inside each other's arms like worms and caterpillars; you kissing me like you'd been getting paid for it all these years and this was your last paycheck; and my head getting lost all over your body. I could still hear your faint cries echoing in my head right there on that concrete. Saw my tongue moistening your chest and your hands rubbing all across and around my back like I was made of silk. I was silk and you knew it. You smelled so damn good. And you never stopped me when my head fell off the bed. You came after it. You never said anything when I screamed and called out your name, just took your time with me and kept pulling me inside your arms, inside the cave of your chest and would not let me go. And when I woke up, you were the dream I thought I had.

And yet, there you were out on that sidewalk in the heat with another girl chained to your arm, walking past my house without a care in the world. This shit burns me up.

I mean, look. You didn't have to make me laugh out loud, tickle me, and change the Band-Aid on my cut thumb, or sniff my hair and tell me it smelled like a cool forest. You didn't have to tell me it didn't matter that my breasts were small, and I was relieved to hear that, cause my mama always told me that a man should be more interested in how you fill his life and not how you fill your bra.

I mean, who told you to show me the puppets you'd made of James Brown and Diana Ross and the Jackson

Five? Who told you to burn jasmine candles and make me listen to twelve old Temptations albums after telling me your favorite one of all was "Ain't Too Proud to Beg?" You didn't have to climb up on a bar stool and drag out your scrapbook and give me the privilege of seeing four generations of your family. Showing me your picture as a little nappy-headed boy. What made you think I wanted to see you as a child when I'd really only known you as a man for three weeks? But no, you watched me turn my key in my front door for two whole months while you walked that little mutt before you allowed yourself to say more than "hello" and "good morning."

I never did get around to explaining myself, did I? I mean, I think I told you I was a special education teacher. I think I told you that once in a while I write poems. Even wrote one for you but I'm glad I didn't give it to you. Your ego probably would've popped out of your chest. But maybe I should've told you about the nights when my head pumps no blood, and about the dreams I have of being loved just so. How I have always wanted to give a man more than a symphony inside and outside the bedroom. But it is so hard. Look at this.

You just should not have wrapped your arms and shoulders around me like I was your firstborn child. You should not have shown me tenderness and passion. Was this just lust? I mean, I wasn't asleep when you kept on touching and rubbing my face like I was crystal and you were afraid I would break. I pretended because I didn't want you to rupture this cocoon I was inside of. So I just let you touch; never wanted you to stop touching me.

Three hours ago I transplanted my plants anyway. I baked three zucchini cakes that cost me almost thirty dollars, but after this morning I cannot picture myself sitting out on those cement steps in the heat trying to sell a piece of cake to total strangers. My roommate said she didn't mind. And I'm not going to sit in this hot house all day and be miserable.

"Wanna meet me for brunch?" I ask a girlfriend. She has no money. "I'll pay, just meet me, girl, okay?" She understands that I'm not really hungry but will eat anything just to take up inside space and get me away from this street.

The block was starting to fill up with makeshift vendors displaying junk they'd pulled out of attics and closets and basements so that they wouldn't have to drag them to the Salvation Army. I could already smell barbecue and pop-corn and hear the d.j. testing his speakers for the highest quality of sound that he could expect to get from outside. It was very hot and the sun was beating down on the pavement, making the heat penetrate through your shoes.

I'm wearing my tightest bluejeans and think I look especially good this afternoon on my way to the train station. I work hard to look good. Not for you or the general public, but for me. Here you come again, strutting toward me with that sissy little dog tagging alongside your big feet, but this time there's nothing on your arm but soft black hair and a rolled-up red plaid shirt sleeve. I can see orchards of black hair peeking out at me from your chest and though my knees want to buckle, I dig my heels deeply into the leather so as to make myself stand up straight like a dancer. You smile at me before we meet face to face and then do one of your about-face turns. Start walking beside me without even being invited.

"Hello," I say, as I make sure I don't lose the pace of my stride I've worked so hard on establishing when I first noticed you.

"My goodness, you *do* look pretty today. Pink and purple are definitely your colors."

I smile because I know I look good and even though I can hardly breathe from holding my stomach in to look its absolute flattest, I don't want you staring at anything on my body too tough because you've seen far too much of it already. I take that back. I want you to be mesmerized by this sight so that you remember what everything looked and felt like underneath this denim because you won't be anywhere near that close again: daytime or nighttime. I move closer to the curb.

"Where you going today?" you ask, showing some real interest. And since I want you to think I'm a very busy woman and that this little episode has not fazed me in the least, I say, "I'm having brunch with a friend." I really wanted to tell you it wasn't any of your damn business, but no, I'm not only polite, but honest.

We walked six hard hot blocks and when we finally reached the subway steps, you bent down like you were about to kiss me, and I stared at your smooth brown lips puckering up as if you had a cold sore on them, and turned my head. You kissed that girl this morning.

"Can I call you later, then?" you asked.

"If the spirit moves you," I said and disappeared underground.

By the time I got home it was almost ten o'clock and the street was still full of teenagers roller-skating, skateboarding, and dancing to the loud disco music blasting from both ends of the block. Kids were running around and through a full-spraying fire hydrant in high shrills of excitement, while grownups sat on the stoops sipping beers and drinks from Styrofoam cups. My roommate was sitting on our stoop and I joined her. Though it was hard to see, I found myself looking for your tall body over all the other smaller ones. When I didn't see you immediately, this disturbed me because I could see your lights on and I knew you couldn't be sitting up in that muggy apartment with all this noise and activity going on down here.

When I saw you leaning against a wrought-iron fence across the street, there was a different girl stuck deep into your side. You spotted me through the thick crowd of teenagers and I heard you call out my name, but I ignored you. I was too proud to let myself feel sad or jealous or anything stupid like that.

My roommate told me she sold exactly three pieces of my zucchini cake because folks were afraid to buy it. Thought it might be green inside. I didn't care about the loss.

I felt spry and spunky, so I kicked off my pink pumps and marched down the steps and walked straight into the fanning water of the fire hydrant along with the kids. The hard mist felt cool and soothing as it fell against my skin. My entire body was tingling as if I had just had a massage. And even though I could feel your eyes following me, I didn't turn to acknowledge them. I sat back down on the steps, wiped the water from my forehead, the hot pink lipstick from my lips, ate a piece of my delicious zucchini cake, and popped the lid on an ice-cold beer. The foam flowed over the top of the bottle and down my fingers. I shook off the excess, and leaned back against the cement steps so it would scratch my back when I rocked from side to side and popped my fingers to the beat.

## Carolyn Forche

# Kalaloch

The bleached wood massed in bone piles,
we pulled it from dark beach and built
fire in a fenced clearing.
The posts' blunt stubs sank down,
they circled and were ropfed by milled
lumber dragged at one time to the coast.
We slept there.

Each morning the minus tide—
weeds flowed it like hair swimming.
The starfish gripped rock, pastel,
rough. Fish bones lay in the sun.

Each noon the milk fog sank
from cloud cover, came in
our clothes and held them
tighter on us. Sea stacks
stood and disappeared.
They came back when the sun
scrubbed out the inlet.

We went down to piles to get
mussels, I made my shirt
a bowl of mussel stones, carted
them to our grate where they smoked apart.
I pulled the mussel lip bodies out,
chewed their squeak.
We went up the path for fresh water, berries.
Hardly speaking, thinking.

During low tide we crossed
to the island, climbed
its wet summit. The redfoots

46

and pelicans dropped for fish.
Oclets so silent fell
toward water with linked feet.

Jacynthe said little.
Long since we had spoken *Nova Scotia,*
*Michigan,* and knew beauty in saying nothing.
She told me about her mother
who would come at them with bread knives then
stop herself, her face emptied.

I told her about me,
never lied. At night
at times the moon floated.
We sat with arms tight
watching flames spit, snap.
On stone and sand picking up
wood shaped like a body, like a gull.

I ran barefoot not only
on beach but harsh gravels
up through the woods.
I shit easy, covered my dropping.
Some nights, no fires, we watched
sea pucker and get stabbed by
the beacon
circling on Tatoosh.

**2**

I stripped and spread
on the sea lip, stretched
to the slap of the foam
and the vast red dulce.
Jacynthe gripped the earth
in her fists, opened—
the boil of the tide
shuffled into her.

The beach revolved,
headlands behind us
put their pines in the sun.
Gulls turned a strong sky.
Their pained wings held,
they bit water quick, lifted.

Their looping eyes continually
measure the distance from us,
bare women who do not touch.

Rocks drowsed, holes
filled with suds from a distance.
A deep laugh bounced in my flesh
and sprayed her.

**3**

Flies crawled us,
Jacynthe crawled.
With her palms she
spread my calves, she
moved my heels from each other.
A woman's mouth is
not different, sand moved
wild beneath me, her long
hair wiped my legs, with women
there is sucking, the water
slops our bodies. We come
clean, our clits beat like
twins to the loons rising up.

We are awake.
Snails sprinkle our gulps.
Fish die in our grips, there is
sand in the anus of dancing.
Tatoosh Island
hardens in the distance.
We see its empty stones
sticking out of the sea again.
Jacynthe holds tinder
under fire to cook the night's wood.

*If we had men I would make
milk in me simply.* She is
quiet. *I like that you
cover your teeth.*

## Patrice Vecchione

# Moving House

The bulk of our bodies moves
under the sheets
in an upstairs bedroom
like a house on wheels.
And the view from the windows
changes each time
we kiss.

Your tongue
slips between my teeth,
my lips pull
on your warm cheek.
All the redness we make
like dark curtains, like blood.
Our sex is burlap, then velvet
as we twist and turn
in the old family house.

We travel
with the dishes rattling
through ranch country,
past the odor of cattle grazing
to the sea and plant the
wooden pillars in the damp earth
we can not keep from sinking.

# Sandy Boucher

# The Game of Chess

The house was a gray Victorian, its façade alive with a montage of styles, from the heavy rhythm and blues of the stone foundation to the country funkiness of its window-box geraniums, to the jazz embellishments of an elaborate scrolled cornice here, a leaded window there, a cupola perched up on top. It had once been a single-family house and now was divided into six small apartments. Ours on the ground floor rear opened onto a tiny grassy backyard. Conrad and Bridget's apartment, just above us, was a two-room cave with sooty walls and torn linoleum on the floor. This floor did little to muffle sound, so that we in our bedroom below were privy to the most intimate moments of their lives, as (I blush to admit) they certainly were to ours.

I first saw Conrad when I came to the house on Divisadero to decide about renting the downstairs apartment for me and my husband John. Arriving a few minutes before the rental agent, I loitered in the lobby, looking around me without enthusiasm, but trying to like what I saw, for John and I had to have a place by the end of the month.

The front door opened and a young man stepped in. He was dressed in jeans and T-shirt, his dark hair in a thick unruly mop down to his shoulders. But it was his eyes that I will never forget. They were black and so fiercely intent upon me that my mouth literally dropped open. Something vibrated down inside me, like a jazz riff, surprising yet familiar in its inevitability. For one brief moment he glanced at me, then with a quick interested hello he brushed past me on the stairs. I turned to see him pause again, looking down on me, his eyes unnaturally shiny in the darkness. The agreement was sealed between us.

It was not hard to convince John that we should rent the apartment, though he grumbled that upper Divisadero was a high-crime area and we would probably be ripped off

50

soon. (In fact, we were, while we lived there, and true poetic justice decreed that the burglars, in each break-in, took only my things and left John's untouched.) I will never forget the look of extreme delight on Conrad's face when he came down the stairs and saw us wrestling boxes through the door.

I was touched by his shyness as he introduced himself as Conrad Klein, shook John's hand, and was careful to glance only briefly into my eyes. Clearing his throat uncomfortably, he offered to help with the boxes, and I noticed that his voice was deep and rough.

He was used to being a muscle man, it was clear, as he easily lifted things that John, who was lanky and thin, had to struggle with. And while he was ill at ease, he obviously enjoyed himself as he carried in box after box. His wide full mouth softened in a smile beneath a narrow nose slightly hooked, flat cheeks and a wide forehead. As I rummaged in boxes, I felt a particular warmth in my chest, a promise.

While his girlfriend Bridget listened to Bob Dylan, Conrad's taste ran to jazz. Lying in bed, John and I were baptized from above by the smooth warm sax of John Coltrane. Then when the record stopped, we heard the pounding and realized it was a bed hitting the wall in quick regular thumps. John and I lay in silence, listening, as Conrad's voice came in louder and louder Ohs. The thumps quickened. It went on for many minutes, and I wondered how he could keep it up, then remembered those beautifully modeled thighs, the tight round buttocks.

I lay there drowning in a rush of sensation, my cunt throbbing, amused and annoyed at once at having to hear this, yet treasuring every moment. And feeling curious and a trifle contemptuous of Bridget, who never uttered a sound, as Conrad's voice burst out in a shout and then all was still.

John and I did not speak of this eavesdropping. What was there to say . . . for our admitting to it would acknowledge the fact that *they* must hear everything *we* did. That was strangely thrilling to me, for unlike Bridget, I was very vocal especially in that last excruciating moment, and I knew that Conrad heard me.

He knew the sounds I made in my most vulnerable, intimate moments. This condition went unremarked between us when he came down to use our phone. (A poor student, he could not afford one of his own.) He came without his shirt. Was he trying to drive me crazy? John and I had been playing chess—a game he had taught me while we were in the Peace Corps in Africa—and after he opened the door to let Conrad in, he came back to the board where it was his move. Pretending to watch John, I looked at Conrad, and I literally felt my nipples go hard under my blouse and the whole front of my body begin to tingle.

He did not look at me as he talked on the phone, but he stood so that I could see his whole torso from the front. His broad shoulders sloped down slightly from a powerful neck, the biceps tight under surprisingly white skin. His breasts were broad plates with dark brown nipples like Hershey's kisses. His jeans hung low on his hips revealing a tender flat belly and curve of hipbone, and above it his torso was ridged with muscle. Such a shy one—what a gift to bring to me here: five minutes of looking at your body. I would lick every inch of you.

"Your move," John said.

Before he left, Conrad expressed interest in our chess game and said he, too, played. John asked him if he would like to play sometime with one or the other of us, and Conrad looked so happy that his eyes shone.

So it began. At least two nights a week he came downstairs. The first game he played with John, but while he did, he and I had a conversation that included John (for it was obvious Conrad liked John heartily and wanted to know him better) but developed a certain level of communication that was meant only for Conrad and myself. I discovered that he was a math student who was crazy about jazz. And it was soon obvious that his inarticulacy extended only as far as small talk and the usual amenities. Where jazz was concerned, he expressed himself with passionate precision. I, for my part, had always listened to a lot of music, and knew what I liked.

From upstairs came the nasal drone of Bob Dylan while Conrad and I disagreed. He admired the spare, modern sound of Albert Ayler, while I thought Ayler was too abstract, too cold. My own taste ran to the passionate, angry strength of Charlie Mingus. Conrad found him "self-indulgent," with "flashes of brilliance," he said, "but undisciplined." Conrad instructed me delicately, without seeming to put me down, that the most complex and experimental music played by black musicians was not to be called jazz but "black classical music," and I was reminded that he was from New York, where such decisions were made.

John, whose taste ran to Joan Baez, soon dropped out of

the conversation to concentrate on the chess game. Without actually point-blank asking about them, I found out about Conrad's muscles. With a certain reluctance, he told me he had played football at his high school in the Bronx and that he now sometimes worked out with weights.

"Checkmate!"

Conrad looked stunned, and then amused, and his eyes raised to mine.

John was pleased. We sat for half an hour, the three of us, drinking coffee, smoking cigarettes, talking about the student strike at San Francisco State College. The strike had been called to pressure the administration into creating a Black Studies department. The Panthers were involved now. It was rough and exciting, and Conrad was in the midst of it. I told him about my picketing in front of Denny's where I went each evening after my secretarial job at an auto-leasing firm downtown. John, who had dropped out of grad school to work with the Head Start program, told Conrad about his joys and frustrations there. The three of us agreed on most things. We would be friends.

Soon it was Conrad and I who played chess. Those evenings we sat across the board from each other, Conrad slumped over, brooding, his eyes like black rabbits darting among the pieces. We smoked without pause, reaching to the side of the board where the ashtray sat. Smoked to stall for time, to go inside, to give our hungry mouths something to do. How I watched his mouth. An upperlip with a little dip in the center, his lower lip lightly moist and shiny. He knew I was looking at him. And when he would allow himself to look into my eyes, we would both stop breathing, then quickly glance down at the chess pieces again. The air between us was so thick with lust that I am surprised it did not ignite when we lit a new cigarette.

Very infrequently, when we both reached for our cigarettes at the same time, our fingertips would touch. That brief contact came like an electric jolt, and for a few moments we were stunned, blanked out, before we could go back to the chess game.

John had taught me to play, as I said, while we were in Africa. We had been working in a remote village where there was, to my sorrow, nothing to plug a phonograph into. On the long steamy evenings we would sit outside our hut, eagerly watched by half the village, and play chess. For the first year I never won a game. John told me that was normal. Now in the third year of our marriage, I won every

other game, at least, and had been known to take two in a
row.

I watched Conrad's hand lift the queen and hold her
above the board. Laced with black hairs at the wrist, his
hand was cleanly defined, broad across the palm with tapered fingers. His nails were always clean and cut straight
across. He lifted my jack out of the queen's way, and sat her
on the jack's square. Then his hand went for his cigarette in
the ashtray and brought it to his mouth. I watched his lips
purse as he inhaled, then the smoke came from his open
mouth where I saw the gleam of regular teeth, the hint of
pink tongue.

Drawing smoke deep into my own lungs, I bent to the
board, staring at the interloping queen, feeling the hot
prickles all over my body that made it seem my skin rippled.
I moved the pawn to threaten his queen, and looked up to
find his eyes on my mouth.

For a whole year—at least two nights a week—we sat over
the chessboard, each time in a state of high arousal, smoking cigarettes, avoiding each others' eyes and fingers. We
listened to the records Conrad brought downstairs, and
now and then I introduced him to something, like a Folk-
ways LP of early jazz in the South that I found in the
library. I watched his buttocks in tight denim as he walked
across the room, and when he turned I would see the bulge
under his zipper, and a hot little hand would open in my
cunt.

Occasionally John and I and Conrad and Bridget would
have dinner together in their apartment or ours. We would
drink beer or red wine, eat spaghetti, maybe smoke a joint,
listen to records. Bridget, who was Southern and extremely
pretty, had a particular technique for relating to men: she
asked them questions and then sat back with big adoring
eyes to hear their answers. These evenings sagged into
boredom as the men lectured on everything from world
affairs to car repair, and I sat locked in irritation. Throughout, Conrad and I were scrupulous in our avoidance of
each other, each of us concentrating on our respective mate.
Bridget rarely glanced in my direction, nor did she ever ask
my opinion on anything.

Conrad and I managed our mutual desire. It was something we carried with us; sometimes it grew huge and un-
wieldy, sometimes it shrank to discreet proportions. We
were waiting. I remember one sunny afternoon when I

went out back to lie in the sun. I lay face down, inhaling the fresh grass smell, enjoying the heat on my bare shoulders. (I was wearing a bathing suit.) Up above, from Conrad's apartment, came his music. Ornette Coleman this time, playing with Paul Bley an intricate interweaving of sounds like sprays of reflected light out over the lawn. Gradually I felt something that made me turn over and look up. There, his big forearms resting on the windowsill, was Conrad. His mouth was open, and his dark eyes held a stunned, dreamy expression. He looked at my body and I was aware of my thighs open, my belly, the skin of my breasts above the bathing suit top marked with pink streaks from the grass. He might as well have been lying with his body on me. It was too much. I turned with a groan and buried my face in the grass.

And night after night John and I heard the thumping upstairs. It would begin as a subtle tapping, a shaking and touching to the wall—pat pat pat pat—and then it got louder and stronger, the ceiling above us beginning to tremble. I imagined him in the bed, on his knees, his body soaked with sweat, thrusting at her, thrusting, pounding. Now his voice came, deep accompaniment to the motion—Oh, oh, oh—rising in volume.

John lay absolutely still, as did I. We had made love earlier ourselves, and this was now a counterpoint. It rose to a wild rattle of thumps and Conrad's voice taking him up over the top. Then that long moan of his completion. And silence.

I do not know if John became as aroused as I did by this performance, but if he did I know there was the tacit understanding that it would be indecent of us to use this for our own titillation and further lovemaking. We lay silent as stones, and my cunt pulsed mightily.

Then one weekend John went away to a Head Start convention in Chicago. He was excited, and both of us regretted that I could not be there to hear him give his presentation. After I took him to the airport I came back to the house just in time to hear the phone ringing. I picked it up, and there was that deep scratchy voice.

"Can I bring down some music?"

I drew in a breath and held it. Then I asked, "Bridget?"

"She left two days ago for Knoxville to see her folks."

I let out the breath and my voice was bright. "Yes, come over. Right away."

That afternoon we listened to one record. Conrad had brought Miles Davis's *Round Midnight*, and I appreciated his gesture, Davis being the middle ground between the two extremes of our tastes. We sat across the room from each other and heard the soft, rich intimate sound of muted trumpet, relaxed and methodical, laying down the tune; piano following behind. We really could not, this time, look at each other, except for shy side glances, as the drums and quiet bass moved in behind the trumpet. Then the sax took over, sexy and cajoling, like a conversation on a sunny streetcorner, the bass and piano commenting, a cymbal clicking behind. Gradually I realized there was no one else in the house but us. No one upstairs waiting, listening. Breathy and warm, the trumpet joined the sax and the two brought it all home.

We stood up and walked toward each other. Even before the next cut began to play I said, "Let's go to the bedroom."

I watched him take off his jeans, revealing a sturdy circumcised cock rising out of a mat of thick hair that was nowhere near as dark as his head hair. As he helped me out of my clothes, I touched his brown chocolate-drop nipples, and he shuddered. His eyes until now had been shiny and dazed. Now he looked up full into my eyes and we both grinned as if our lips would split.

The next hour I remember only in snatches, moments of clarity like little bright islands of trumpet solo in a gentle river of bass and piano, tender and deep all at once.

The counterpoint of the next song, "Ah Leu Cha," sax and trumpet prodding each other, then the trumpet taking control, tipping over into the notes, reeling them out in spirals. His cock hard against my pubis. I reach down, striking his side as I go and slip his penis between my thighs, so that its length presses up against my vagina. Now our mouths meet and we kiss as if our whole bodies were in our mouths, yet at the same time I feel every inch of my skin touching his. Our heat ignites me. I move my hips ever so slightly, his cock imprisoned by my thighs.

An instant in which I stare at the ceiling, and wonder, Is he *really here* with me? Not upstairs? The drum and piano answer, making a strong grid on which the sax dances like a drop of mercury.

\*          \*          \*

His dark head there between my thighs, his tongue probing.

Piano takes over, celebrating with fans and necklaces of notes, as I move my lips over his chest, teasing the brown nipple into hardness. Kiss, and stroke his chest with one hand, hold his cock in the other. Swollen, hard, almost throbbing with readiness. But he lets me explore him, brush his belly with my lips, even lean to take his furry balls in my mouth. The smell of him! Sweat and a sweet/sharp sex smell.

Sax and trumpet tangle in sinewy scrolls of sound. Above me arches his body, his thighs tensed on either side of my face, his penis and balls a few inches from me. I reach up with one hand to stroke the cock, caress the balls. He is groaning with pleasure, vibrating his tongue in and out of my hot open cunt. I am moving, moaning. And now I want his cock in my mouth. I pull it down and take it, sucking, moving up and back on its shaft. It tastes wonderfully of him. I am so close to orgasm that I am delirious.

Miles is way off now, stepping gracefully, suave as a dancer in cocked fedora, through the easy turns of "All of You." He's so far away, as Conrad's face appears above me, his wild eyes glazed over. And his cock comes into me. We both cry out. I want him, all of him, in me. He fucks me then, at first slowly, as I knew he would, his eyes burning down into mine, while I stroke his chest, turn to suck his wrist braced next to my head. Then faster and faster, as with each thrust I feel the cradle of his pelvis holding me, the shaft of his penis penetrating deep.

Our voices sound together, loud and jubilant and conquered.

We hear the trumpet, so relaxed, oiled with the familiarity of this old tune, that had been there behind us all the time, like daily life, like the sax now, sweet, mulling it over, touching it and playing with it and then giving it over to the piano. Conrad's voice vibrates in his throat as he says, "Oh, I am so *glad.*"

That is all either of us said until night had filled the room and our stomachs growled, and we had heard that record fifty times. Then we got up to eat. I remember him sitting there nude on a kitchen chair, eating a hamburger, his cock limp against one hairy thigh, his face dreamily smiling at me.

That whole weekend we stayed in bed, making love and resting, smoking and making love, not talking much. On Sunday evening he went upstairs, and I left to drive to the airport to pick up John.

Two weeks later he left for the East Coast, his parting visit made uneasy by John's presence. But the bond between us has never been broken. We have seen each other two times in the last twenty years, both times in circumstances where we could only shout across a distance at one another. But at least twice a year there is a letter from him, about his job, his wife and children, the music he likes now. And I write to him of things I never tell anyone else, knowing he will receive my confessions with love, knowing that he is glad I am alive in this world with him.

As for the game of chess, I gave it up. It didn't hold much interest for me after a while. My present husband would raise his eyebrows in astonishment if I suggested we play chess. But I wouldn't anyway. Who could possibly match Conrad as a partner? So uniquely challenging. And satisfying.

# Rosemary Daniell

# Talking of Stars

Talking softly of stars
we lie within our beds.

Nausea pulses my throat—
galaxies make me faint,
thinking how we float—
light things in shadowy
sheets.
   Later, wakening
from dreams of peacock wings

fluttered to dust ten thousand
years ago, I move through
quiet doors. In darkness,
my back presses the shivery
earth—
   with the old bone of
an animal, I love myself.

# Yuri Kageyama

# Eros

The silk-woven clouds streaming through the folds of her kimono catch at her kicking calves, wrap and unwrap her thighs that are already flushing in their wait for the contact of his touch.

The dry leaves, red tinged and yellow streaked, pieces of paper made from rice, hiss beneath her zoris, then fly up behind her, as though suddenly alive with the same wildness that breathes inside her.

She pants high in her throat, for her stomach is heavy, pushing against her diaphragm. Her hands move to her lower abdomen, rubbing the tightly stretched skin, helping to lift the weight.

Stopping where bending branches sway low, discarding leaves into a soft circle of grass, soft and circular from the white light, drifting visible rays like a whisper, she arches her back, half groaning, half sighing.

She squints toward the direction he is expected.

She knows he will come, he always has, but the lurk of a fear palpitates in her belly, in rhythm with the stranger's kicks, the movements of the little one growing sheltered within her, who, she is certain, is waiting as anxiously as she is, for the man's arrival.

Each time she sees his face—no matter that she had done it time and time again—an excitement flickers in her heart, catching the light that emanates from his face (for, as the ancient texts have it, fine men glow in their splendor), with another fear that she is unworthy of him. Especially now. She is bloated, deformed. She is ashamed of how her hips have spread, her bones magically pliant for the passage of new life.

But he is lifting her face in his two palms that feel dry like the leaves.

Then, kneeling, he places his ear and cheek next to her stomach, smiles when he draws back from a vicious kick.

He pulls her to him, holds her tight, her melting into his robe, immersed by his alien male scent.

Nothing else matters. She forgets to feel.

He is afraid his entering may hurt the child.

Nevertheless, the temporary intimacy, the prying, intrigues him. He wonders if, through layers of numbing flesh and rubbery waters, his tip is nudging the soft spot on the still-to-be-born's head, and if he or she resents the intrusion as a mild annoyance or as a true discomfort.

The woman feels warmer.

Her insides have changed, as though there were an added redness.

# Sharon Olds

# New Mother

A week after our child was born,
you cornered me in the spare room
and we sank down on the bed.
You kissed me and kissed me, my milk undid its
burning slip-knot through my nipples,
soaking my shirt. All week I had smelled of milk,
fresh milk, sour. I began to throb:
my sex had been torn easily as cloth by the
crown of her head, I'd been cut with a knife and
sewn, the stitches pulling at my skin—
and the first time you're broken, you don't know
you'll be healed again, better than before.
I lay in fear and blood and milk
while you kissed and kissed me, your lips hot and swollen
as a teenage boy's, your sex dry and big,
all of you so tender, you hung over me,
over the nest of stitches, over the
splitting and tearing, with the patience of someone who
finds a wounded animal in the woods
and stays with it, not leaving its side
until it is whole, until it can run again.

# Jill Jeffery Ginghofer

# Domestic Love

Trapped in their high chairs in the kitchen, the twins of two and a half were flicking balls of wet cereal at one another, the walls, the windows. Joan had often thought of boiling the dining area and sending the residue to China, but a recent TV documentary had revealed that the Chinese were well fed. Perhaps I should send it to India, Joan thought as she wiped their good-natured faces, lifted them out of their high chairs. Joan brushed another milk trail from her once elegant black housecoat and started to clear Murray's breakfast dishes. She smiled as she thought of his morning ritual of kissing her good-bye. He went to work in his painting studio, a building only twelve yards behind the house.

"Surprise. Crack o' dawn surprise." A wide-mouthed face with a hand shading the eyes peered through the kitchen window.

"Hi, Vanessa," Joan grinned. "Where's Dylan?"

"I've left him in the car. We're going to story-telling hour at the library. Would the twins like to come?"

"They'll never sit still," Joan protested, but the twins were already scrambling around in their bedroom for clothes.

"See you in a couple of hours," Vanessa shouted from her car. The twins, sitting sedately on the back seat, waved to Joan dutifully, as if they were leaving a distant relative.

Two hours alone! Amazing. I haven't been alone in the house since before the twins' birth, Joan thought. Or was it Zoe's four years ago? If she rushed through the housework she would have time for a shower and then, ecstasy, time to lie on her bed and read a book. Perhaps even to nap. No, she dare not nap for fear she forget to collect Zoe from nursery school at twelve.

She ran from kitchen, to bedroom, to laundry, then back

to the kitchen again. At times the house seemed almost sinister in the silence, in the sense of something vital missing. She chanted firmly to herself, "Zoe is safe at nursery school. The twins are safe with Vanessa. Murray is in the studio and with luck will stay there all morning. Everything is all right and I am alone."

Her work finished, Joan moved softly through the quiet house to the bathroom. She threw off her housecoat and the shabby nightgown she had taken to wearing for warmth when the children woke her at night. As she leaned forward to turn on the water, she moved into a gentler pace, into a world in which she was the central object.

From the window in the bath stall she could see the mass of climbing nasturtiums that engulfed the camellia and bella donna bushes. Occasionally a drop of water on her eyelashes came into vision and momentarily the garden was trapped, convex and minute, before she blinked and a hundred tiny gardens scattered. The water flowed over her, soothing her aching neck and shoulders.

Turning in the protective curtain of water, she was startled by the sound of the back door clicking open. Blast! Who was that? She heard the familiar footsteps in the kitchen, felt the water pressure drop for an instant—Murray filling the kettle. There was a scrape as he put the kettle on the stove. He was probably making some tea. His steps moved out of the kitchen, but there was no click of the back door.

Damn! She knew he was listening to the silence. He was also hearing the shower running. She could guess what he was thinking. There were no children in this house and soon there will be a steam-hot woman naked with creams in the bathroom. She heard his footsteps, this time fast and purposeful. The back door closed, then seconds later there was the scrape of the studio door. He had gone to make sure the painting was at a place where he could leave it, to put his brushes in turpentine.

If I'm fast, she thought, I could be dry, dressed, and appear to be doing something useful before he came back in. She turned the water off, twisted a towel around her wet hair and 'reached for another to dry herself. A low whistle started to fill the house, becoming increasingly shrill. She had to turn the kettle off before he heard it in the studio. She flew, the towel held in front of her, past the twins' bedroom, through the living room to the kitchen, turned off the gas, and was racing back when she heard the scrape of the studio door. Oh Lord! He mustn't see her. She leaned into Zoe's bedroom off the far side of the living room, pressed herself against the wall behind the open door, and held her breath.

He took three steps into the house, then stopped. From where he stood he could see the gas under the kettle was off. She imagined him with his head cocked, thinking. With measured tread he walked past the open door of Zoe's room, through the living room, past the twins' room to the bathroom. Silence. She heard the far door that led from the bathroom through a hallway~ to their bedroom open and close. Quickly she looked around for somewhere to hide, but the floor of Zoe's room was strewn with clothes, books, skates, records, dolls. Crunching through all that rubbish to try squeezing under the bed could make too much noise. She shook her head, chagrined at her own and her daughter's untidiness.

Oh no. He was coming back. The bathroom door clicked open again. There was a long silence. He was taking his time to survey the bathroom, noticing her gown draped over the stool. No doubt adding up the fact that she had to be somewhere in the house, and naked. A board creaked in the twins' room. He was taking a good look around in there too. Quietly and firmly she pressed her hand against the door, carefully pushing it. It moved an inch, then two, then stopped. She felt resistance. Peering through the narrow crack between door and wall, she saw that a leg from Zoe's toy ironing board, which was on its side on the floor, was caught between the door and the lintel.

She heard him pad into the living room. She stopped breathing, her eyes wide in her head, praying the door was not still moving. She jumped as the wall creaked behind her and dark appeared in the crack by the door hinge. Oh, God. It was his thumb. He was leaning on the other side of the wall. She felt her stomach surge, a hot sinking. "My beloved put in his hand by the hole of the door and my bowels were moved for him." Where did that come from? Solomon. The Songs.

Now where was he? She heard something brush against the back of the sofa. Still in the living room. She could almost hear him thinking. Silence. The loose board in the twins' room snapped softly. As if in a dream she could see through the tangle of roses outside the window of Zoe's room, across their large yard, and down to the road where in the distance a neighbor and his son were bending under the hood of a car, their smudged faces reappearing from time to time for consultations. This is absurd, she thought. What am I doing here? Where's Murray?

Perhaps he had given up. That was it. He had decided to go back to the studio through the French windows in the bedroom. That meant he would pass the windows of this room any second now. She dropped to her knees and quietly as she could started crawling, her knees crunching sharply on Legos, crayons, toward the darkest corner of the house.

A door clicked in the house. She was up and back behind the door in two steps, panting, her heart pounding wildly.

She heard him in the bathroom, turning a faucet so tightly it squeaked. He could be very angry by now. Why didn't he give up? The snap of the board in the twins' room. Silence. It snapped again. Was he going back out to their bedroom? The listening was painful, a taut humming wire between her ears. Her shoulders, covered in goose bumps, pressed forward in the effort. There was a soft creak from the living room. Her eyes peered through the slit by the door hinge. There he was, frozen mid-stride in the center of the room, silent, head cocked, straining. It's as if we are both animals, she thought, listening for fate to move. He glided quietly out of her narrow view.

The scrape of a chair on the tile floor in the dining area. The fridge door opened, then closed. She knew it was habit that made him look in there whenever he was in the kitchen. Again, silence. So intent was she on listening, it felt as if she were drawing air in through her ears.

Suddenly a high whine split the air. She jumped, her thoughts flying, trying to place the brain-splitting noise. It was a machine of some kind. Then she remembered. The couple across the street had threatened to cut down a grove of eucalyptus trees, afraid they would collapse on their house. Why were they doing this now?

Abruptly, the chain saw stopped. The silence was startling, as if the world had ceased turning. She could not hear a thing now, the machine's whine still echoing in her ears. Her back felt intolerably exposed.

She looked up. Murray was staring at her, leaning around the door, a thoughtful expression in his eyes, a forefinger crooked, beckoning. Slowly she straightened, drawing the towel up against her breasts. She could feel the heat of him from where she stood, pulling her forward, drawing her own heat south, sucking her into the blackberry-dark heart of her marriage.

## Carol Staudacher

# Beginning to Love Again, in the Middle of My Life

Do you know how it grieves me
that you have seen me so many times
with my face swollen shut like a clock,
brain ticking behind eyes slugged in sockets
and wishing away the circles for your sake?

If only you could have known me
when I had eyes that were fresh,
not bludgeoned and burdened
into a tired editor's stare.
If only you could have known me
when I rode high in the night making love
and my hair beat like a blond flag in victory
on a back that was trembling and bare
when skin kept close to muscle and bone
and turned a formidable gold every summer.

Now older, I face you and touch you
and everything in me descends to an underground forest
for growing unused and unusual cries.
You say the beauty I see now in your eyes
is because of me looking; but still,
don't discount it. It is not any look
I remember having before.

And when I take you between me,
when I press us together and push my pulse
to your veins, will you feel us ticking delicately
backward together, yet forward in fury
to be less than we ever have been before—
but with a new name, and in a new skin
even more?

# Valerie Miner

# Excerpt from Winter's Edge

The dome clock chimed eight. The doorbell made it nine.

Ever punctual. Margaret imagined he had to be prompt after a life of giving services. You can't do Sunday without the minister. She liked the consideration he showed to her and others. Pausing before Grandma's mirror, she fluffed out the back of her hair. Time for another henna already, quite disappointing. She switched down one of the lamps. Good. A nice soft light. She had given up trying to hide her wrinkles—had even come to like the ones around her eyes. Still, she was proud of this dark hair. Chrissie urged her to "go natural." What was natural about gray when she had been coal black all her life?

He was carrying something. Not flowers, Margaret noted, a bottle.

"Cognac." He spoke awkwardly. "Given to me after a wedding last week. A man can't drink on his own, so I thought I'd share it with my favorite friend." He kissed her cheek.

Slocum barked sharply. Getting no response from Margaret, she skulked into the kitchen and lay down heavily next to her bowl.

Graciously, Margaret accepted the bottle, cautioning herself to remember the night of the martini and to proceed slowly.

"I'm afraid I don't have," she stumbled, "anything to go with it."

"You have glasses," he grinned. "And me."

She offered him a seat and walked into the kitchen, unnerved that the evening was already going a little too fast for her.

His long, tapered fingers held the brandy glass as if it were a chalice. His baritone voice was certainly itself. She had a hard time believing their intimacy, believing she wasn't really still in the back pew daydreaming.

He was telling her how he had talked a man from jumping off the St. Francis Hotel four years ago. How he had stayed with the man twelve hours. Yes, Margaret knew, she had read the story in the *Chronicle*. In fact, it was this incident that started her going to church again. She wasn't much interested in what religion could do for you in the next world. It seemed more important that she could enjoy this one first. And if Roger Bentman could talk somebody into life, she would try his church.

Slocum crept quietly into the room.

Relaxing back on the couch, Margaret moved her stockinged feet through Slocum's fur. She watched Roger's lips. She breathed in the sweet, fruity smell of the cognac and savored his voice.

Abruptly, he slid closer. "You live so attentively." He looked at her and then took a long sip.

"Pardon?" She was at once disappointed by the end to their meditative stillness and excited by his closeness. She reminded herself that he was a man of God, that her urges were premature.

"I often watch your face when I preach. You're always following. Sometimes you're ahead of me."

"Ahead?" Margaret asked, putting down the brandy with distress. She had only taken a sip or two. She watched Slocum move back to the kitchen.

"An inspiration." He took her hand.

She felt such fondness. She knew they would kiss next. Carefully, she took in the smile on his lips, the gray in his eyes. He set down the glass and drew her toward him. This was like their first kiss, after the theater, and the other since. Gentle, sweet, sure. Yet, now there was something else, something deeper and more urgent. She was conscious of his sweat, of the warmth of his breath, of the loosening in her own body. He held her more closely and she reached her arms around his back as if he were a lifeguard pulling her from the ocean. *Rye beach in July, Mom chasing Pop across miles of umbrellas, sand in her fist, ready to throw it, Pop laughing. She and Sylvia watching from their striped towel, understanding that for the moment they must stay with the picnic basket and the wallets, must play parents while Mom and Pop run through the sand.*

"Margaret," he startled her. "Margaret, I love you, I do."

She drew back and searched his eyes.

"Ever since Florence passed on," he whispered, "I mean since I recovered from her death, I've been aware of you, your attentiveness at service, your cheerfulness in the shop, I . . ."

Margaret moved forward and kissed him again, partially from wanting him and partially from fear of hearing more. Man of God. Body of man.

They held each other for a long time, kissing, rocking, staring with shyness, astonishment, and hunger.

"Dear one," Roger murmured. He took her hand, leading her from the couch. He managed to pull down the Murphy bed with such dispatch that she later understood he must have been planning this movement for weeks.

Deftly he unbuttoned her yellow blouse. She remembered how sex felt as a girl of sixteen—fumbling, breathlessness, guilt, hurry—and she was glad to be seventy years old. Here was a man seasoned in eros, softly rolling his palm over the nylon slip until her nipples hardened, carefully removing the skirt, reaching up between her thighs to find her moistness and then pulling back, allowing her to unbutton his shirt, to kiss the sleek gray hairs on his chest, to move her hand beneath the waistband of his pants and to touch the hard tenderness that had risen for her. She wished it might end here. She had always liked the beginning best, the promise.

He continued to surprise her, tugging down the strap of her slip with his teeth, touching her nipples first with his tongue. Biting gently, licking, biting, licking, biting, lick-bitelickbite in a rhythm she thought might transport her to the ceiling. She was stretching in pleasure before she had a chance to be embarrassed by the folds of age gathered around her body. Gently again, he pulled the slip over her head and removed her pants. She reached down to touch him and found he had shed his clothes, like a lizard might slip from unserviceable skin. They lay side by side touching and stroking.

Circles. Round, wet circles on her belly. The belly of Janey and Rob and Michael. She often forgot it was her belly too. Round and round and round and round and down until he was inside her with his tongue, his wet hungry tongue reaching deep into her body, his thumb making music on her clitoris. Yes, this man was a caretaker. And bolder than she could have hoped. The blue spark of it all astonished her. Electric came the aftershocks: one, two, three, like the last earthquake. He kissed her full on the labia. She drew him on top. He entered her—oh, the satisfaction of this linking—and they rocked until they reached separate peaks.

Afterward (How much later? Impossible to tell from night outside the window. For the downtown night was always stolen by neons and auto horns. Had she slept? Had he slept?) sometime afterward, he turned to her and said, "I love you, Margaret." She looked in his eyes and nodded, watching him fall off to sleep, wondering when she might have to answer.

## Flora Durham

# Shih Ho: Biting Through

The woman has salted the sheets
with sandalwood powder, a remembrance.
A candle stammers, lame and persistent.
The covers lie smooth and clean.

She takes up little space.
She does not know what to ask for
and she has forgotten many things.
She cannot sleep.

Arching and crying out, she dresses
her fingers in her secret smell.
The moon behind rough curtains
is impartial, halved, a thing bitten through.

In the room adjacent, tiny creatures
chatter to each other, caged animals
whose precise teeth natter on wooden bars.
They are planning their escape.

Crescents of nipped wood mount up.
The pregnant housecat licks her swollen teats.

# Rocking the Earth

# Judith W. Steinbergh

# May Day

I wanna call you all the names, baby honey, sweet love, darling, sugarpie, rosehips, apricot lips, I wanna laugh so it's so far down in my belly you feel it through your lovable dick up through your groin until your epiglottis wags with joy, hey honey, don't need no lunch when I got you, don't need no bath, the odors we put out has them formin lines to see what we got cookin, everything comin out of our kitchen, hot and earthy stew, epicurean soufflé, long island duckling even, give me your leg, you take the delicate rise near my breast, this is the first of may and if it wasn't rainin so hard, we'd be lovin it up under that tree, you know the one with its fingers on the ground and the whole earth'd be pushin up against that perfect ass of yours, pine needles stickin in your crack, smells we'd longed for all the winter, dirt on my knees, worms wonderin what the fuss is over- head, everything steamy as if an eruption were imminent, our mouths busy planting and in our heads, the crops, corn, alfalfa, jungles of beans applauding our recognition of the day.

## Elisa Adler

# Let's Make Jazz

Let's make jazz, you and me.
You'll go around talking and laughing
and I'll hop beside you and dance
like your rooster in the morning.

Winter's gone. Swallows swoop in the barn.
Blackbirds in the field are settling
and taking off, singing.
And the wind blows the dandelions—just so.
Shadows
and shimmering cottonwood leaves
dazzle our hazy blue noon.

Dance with me. Let's go!
The chickens are cooing
strutting, clucking around the barnyard.
And tulips, erect and red
bathe in sunlight under the oak tree.

I've got eggs in my pockets,
wind in my feathers.
Come on! Let's go.

# Gina Covina

# There Are Flowers for Everyone in These Hills

There are flowers for everyone in these hills. There are flowers, in May, to suit every fancy. There are monkey flowers, and butter and eggs; Chinese houses and purple nightshade; redwood sorrel and colt's foot and mule's ear and goat's beard. There are twenty-five different clovers in residence in Sonoma County, though they may not all be in flower today. There are milk maids and sugar scoops and sun cups and angelica. There are Solomon's seals both slim and fat, and false Solomon's seal as well. There are rare flowers: the redwood lily, the lady's slipper, the stream orchis, the ghost-white phantom orchid. For the moon and the moody there are baneberry, witches' teeth, skullcap. There is death camas looking like the edible wild onion. There is Ithuriel's spear. There is Diogenes' lantern.

In the hills the fairies are at their most active, dancing in the flowers night and day, ensouling each bloom as it moves from bud to bee-food. Zorra Beth wanders the deer trails in sunlight, picking bouquets for the table, for the outhouse, for her mother's beauty salon. She wears white, these days, and walks barefoot. Fern fronds and meadow foam make a crown in her hair. Frank O'Flanrahan sees her as he comes into the hills with a big basket to pick wild greens for the dinner salad. They wind their ways across the hillside slowly, like forager bees making as many stops as there are flowers. They pass each other twice, three times, gathering.

Buttercup, brodiaea, blue-eyed Mary. Shepherd's purse, plantain, chickweed, dock. Zorra Beth walks softly; she sniffs a dozen flowers for every one she touches; she touches many before picking one. Frank holds a sharp knife, and the basket on his arm. He crouches and cuts, walks and crouches, cuts and gazes—at the bright sky, at the new green, at the floating cloud hem of Zorra Beth's dress, passing.

Bees are working the flowers. Honeybees and bumblebees and sugar bees and little flies. The bees' honey stomachs are full; the back legs of the pollen gatherers hang down heavy-weighted. Zorra Beth's heart floods the hillside with her particular yellow-white joy. Frank feels it, watching her; his own blue-white light spreads through Zora Beth's yellow, making a green-white that could easily be mistaken for the souls of the springtime plants, rising. Frank catches Zorra Beth's eye, and they pause a moment to look into each other. Neither one holds anything back; neither one smiles.

California poppy provides the thick scattered orange, and the texture of silk. Bush monkey flower brings in yellow, and velveteen. Vetch and lupine color the hillside in violets that slide from pale pink to deep purple. Blue-eyed grass reflects the sky; yarrow holds up stalks of white; buttercups mirror the sun, and Indian paintbrush flings bright red across the meadow—all of this shimmering on the deep green of May, all of it alive with bees and butterflies, all shimmering, all alive. Frank stashes his knife and basket of greens in the shade of a bush lupine, and spreads himself into a dish of the meadow, arms out wide and face to the blue. He doesn't see Zorra Beth set her flowers down beside his basket; he doesn't hear her bare feet moving through the green. He doesn't see her reach down to catch the hem of her dress in her hands; doesn't see her stretch her arms over her head and remove the dress in one smooth gesture; doesn't hear the white cotton drop to the ground. Frank doesn't know she is there until she is stretched out along his length, suddenly, all her warm weight pressing into him, her skin dazzling white in the sunlight, her breath on his chin, her bright small eyes on his.

"Zorra Beth." It is all he can say, and softly, as his hands slowly move along the curving warmth of her skin.

Zorra Beth doesn't say anything. Not one small joke, not one witty sentence, not even a murmured sentimental endearment or a giggle at the surprise in Frank's eyes. She doesn't even smile. She sits up, straddling him, and begins to unbutton his shirt. Slowly, all of it slowly, with the May sun warm across her back and framing her face in gold as the light catches in her hair.

A bee works in the clover an inch from Frank's left ear. A small black ant crosses Zorra Beth's foot. Frank watches a translucent pale spider pause at Zorra Beth's shoulder, as she reaches to pull off his shoes; as she turns back, to unzip his pants, the spider slants off into the meadow sun, following some invisible thin thread of its own making. Frank lifts his hips so Zorra Beth can pull off his trousers. There are flowers for everyone in these hills.

## Irene Marcuse

# This Year I Can't Complain

I'm green as grass, as strong
season after season
aching for the sun, the rain

Fullness between my thighs
nipples popping
Calloused hands on round hips
every touch embraces

Garden beds double-dug
soft, inviting sleep
I plant corn and beans
drumming on the earth

Sky melting crimson
first thin slice of moon
and I have bled

Who is this woman
who needs so much
Wants more, always more
fallen, fallen laughing I am

Green horizon line
space between my bones
cracked wide

Pouring out poppies
clouds of lupine
Desire, the juice we feed on

I'm open, open
the moon swells
can't close myself

# *Wendy Rose*

## Frontispoem: Lost Copper

Time to tend the fields again
where I laid my bone-handled spade to earth
and dug from its dirt the shy childsongs
that made my mouth a Hopi volcano.
My hands retreat dusty and brown
there being no water pure enough
to slide the ages and stones from my skin
there being no voice strong enough
to vibrate the skin and muscle apart.
Like a summer-nude horse I roll on my back
and fishtail my hips from side to side;
then on my belly, my navel gone home,
I scrape my cheek and teeth and ride.
From there I rise of earth and wind
to the height of one woman
and cup my breast to the hollow-gourd vine
to feel the place that has sent me songs
to grow from the ground that bears me:
this then my harvest

squash-brown daughters,
blue corn pollen,
lost copper.

# Ann Zoller

# The Privacy of Corn

It was always like this—
the movement of corn, stalks
twisting independently, symphonies
unto themselves, not needing
one another, moving a separate song.

   Dark mornings
I rose at four o'clock
to fix bologna sandwiches
for the trip to fields,
de-tasseling corn that stood overhead
like a green witch.
Yellow pollen clouds above,
pollen picking my neck.
The corn was forever that summer.
Fifty kids in a dump truck
in our fathers' long-sleeve shirts
and faded pants, our skin guarded
from corn leaves grainy as cows' tongues.
Weeks in Iowa fields reaching for tassels
that pointed to the sky like tails of bulls
who run before a storm.
Once after lunch when a morning rain
made the fields thick, I heard them:
the crew boss and Sonja,
their sounds thumping over clods,
through the rows. I stopped,
I think, to be sure and even though
I held my breath and wished it wasn't real,
I knew before words formed.
Their love vibrated the air heavy from rain.
She stretched on the grassy rise at row's end,
the creek beyond, water lazy with leaves

gathered on spindly weeds.
I wanted to turn back
start new rows away, pulling tassels,
one side then the other, working
in rhythm with the massive stalks
but I couldn't, instead I crouched
and waited, my blood burning,
gnats hovered, speckling the sky.
Lying together, their clothes
underneath for a blanket.
His hand traced patterns on her milky skin
and sun through the oak dappled his white back
in a design of shadows. The rolling
tension of the bodies sifted across the knoll
and the corn folded itself around my head,
leaves rustling long sighs.
I remember the sticky pollen on my neck
how my eyes stung from dust,
how sweat ran on my legs.
She turned her head to the side,
not using her eyes but seeing something
distant. A look spread over her
as he arched his back,
as though he were an eagle
lifting the two of them to some cloud close by.
He leaned to the ground,
his back to earth until she rode him
like a leaf at the crest of a tree.
He laughed, suddenly, and the noise
careened over the corn to me,
the laugh spilling with the sun's throb.

We shared the privacy of corn,
each alone, striving for ourselves,
our nakedness opening into earth.
The corn moved through the hot afternoon.
Leaves in the creek broke loose from weed fingers,
floated the current and left.
I turned to the rows, yanking tassels
until time began again. Pollen
caked in my palms, the Iowa heat,
sun homing on me like a white pigeon.

       And after work
the truck bumped into town.

We ordered 51 nickel root-beers
at the A & W. I gulped the sharp drink,
The sting not enough,
my throat still closed.
Secrets of corn moved inside,
a different green now,
vibrant and clean.

# Helen Ruggieri

# An Encounter in Muse, PA.

He sees the sign. "Hey, let me out here," he says. He steps down from the truck into the soft macadam street. Not far away Tabitha is soaking herself in her aunt's clawfoot bathtub. Johnny Adam is watching from the attic window next door. It's hot, sweat runs down his face. He hears sirens and the terrible fear spreads through him. He changes the tempo, takes the rhythm boom boom boom badada da da da da da, the opening of "In the Mood." He begins to dance, shuffling the old jitterbug with an imaginary partner.

Saul steps in the August sun of Muse, PA. He looks around wondering why in hell he stopped here, taking in the empty heart of Muse, PA. He walks past Eratos Bar, a grocery store, an empty store. He walks under the maple shade on broken sidewalks, he walks past a gray house with a wrought-iron fence, past the house with the wooden swing on the porch, hears the scuffling rhythm of Johnny's dance, he walks on. He is trying to remember something, a return address on an envelope, something he saw or heard long ago, something about Muse, PA. Distracted, he continues down the street, finds himself past the town, at the edge of town where fields of wild mustard, ragweed, Aaron's rod, goldenrod, wild purple asters, Michaelmas daisies, stretch away on either side of the road. A pickup truck passes him and stops up ahead, pulling off onto the berm. The door opens, a long splendid leg stretches out, followed by its match. Perfectly shaped, he is thinking, as a sculptor might have done, almost too perfect to be flesh.

A tube top in bright yellow barely covers two large breasts, the cleavage between dark like a cave into destiny. Long black hair coils on her shoulders. He sees her smile, the glinting blue eyes, and staggers toward her, compelled by her bright smile, the teeth so perfect, slightly pointed, animallike. Desire gathers around him, he bites his lip with the

84

pain of it. She leans her head back and laughs softly. He is fascinated as her breasts shake against their bright yellow binder. He reaches out and takes them, one filling, completely and perfectly, each hand. She puts her hands on his chest. He moves her backward until they stand waist deep in the flowers of the field. He pulls the top to her waist gasping at the sun-starred nipples quivering toward him, and lays her down in the wild flowers, seed and pollen dropping on them, sticking to their sweaty bodies as they come together, her nipples cutting into him, his prick reaching for her full of his self-denial, rage, and such desire as men must know facing their deaths. As he enters her the sun falls behind the hills to the west and twilight covers them. Her bright teeth take hold of him, seeming to caress him carefully, the ivory sharpness a risk, their touch the stroke of an artist's brush. Into her he urges all his tenderness and fear and she takes him into herself, holding him, her breath searing him, whispering into his ear an old song, a song he almost remembered, as the heat of her cunt, his own cold fear, the force of her hold, his struggle to penetrate, past the sharp teeth, the need for caution, the need to satisfy, to take her, to free himself, to touch the place where ecstasy waits, aware of the slow shuddering of his body, her soft song, the need to keep his head, the fatal desire to lose it.

It was dark when he woke, his head on her lap, his nose tickled by the black coiling hair, the damp earthy smell of her. Her breasts hang over him almost shutting out the stars. He feels his prick rising, sees the moon rising, silhouetting the perfect curve of her breasts. "Who are you?" he asks. She bends over him taking his prick in her mouth, the heat of it startling, soothing. Her breasts hang in his face. He takes a nipple in his mouth and a rich sweet milk fills it. He feels he is being smothered, tries to pull away, she holds him tightly. He swallows to keep from drowning, relaxing into the sweetness of it, the warmth. It is good. He begins to glow with a strange fire rising from his belly. He hears her murmuring over him and contentment floods him, the thick milky fluid from her breasts trickles out of his mouth, warming his chest. He hiccups and she croons to him, patting his back, the milk still flowing, rolling down his chest, puddling in the hair between his legs, swelling back with tenderness, parting her lips with his hand, the milk on them glowing phosphorescent in the darkness. She seems to glow, too, as if the moon bleached her, the moon or the

milk. The top of his prick is white with milk, hers or his, he
does not know. It glows like a star. He enters slowly, the
incredible softness and heaviness, the sucking sensation, like
entering a whirlpool, a riptide, pulling him in. He fights to
retain control, reciting multiplication tables, trying to concentrate on anything but the fascination of desire until he
touches the certainty of her knowing and in spite of self
comes riding her like a mare to the sun and she with him,
her wild trembling a series of feathers caressing, a set of
tentacles sucking, a million cilia beating him until lost from
life in the ecstasy of St. Vitus, rolling over and over,
weightlessly, effortlessly, bliss and on and on until numbers
have no meaning and death is his pleasure throbbing in her
as a life beyond this plane, and one with her was the knowledge of time, his own death and resurrection, and on and
on they rode the starry night.

He wakes up with the sunrise and she is gone. He lies
there remembering until the sun is high. He stands up
finally, covered with pollen from Aaron's rod, he stands
transformed, a golden man shimmering in the light. He
walks slowly down to a small creek at the end of the field
and after a time, reluctantly, washes himself.

Saul catches a ride at a truck stop on Route 70. He thinks
about what happened in the goldenrod and knew it was the
only real thing that had ever happened to him. That it was
not a dream, perhaps a vision as the old seers told, knowing
it was not real, could not be, yet was. They had not both-
ered with explanations, they accepted the contradictions,
told it for what it was worth to those who would listen, and
held it to themselves like an amulet, letting themselves back
into it like a swimmer entering the water, having it all come
back, smell, touch, everything. He closes his eyes as the
truck rushes southward and they walk down into the field,
his hands over her breasts, she with her hands over his
nipples, she pulling him, he pushing her, like an ancient
courting dance, they move into the golden field, the rank
smell of weeds crushed under them, the sound of bees in
the golden flowers, the cry of pain, seeming to come from
someone else, his, as she closes over him, eyes rolled back,
the empty white eyes of those who have known the lush
contradictories of such encounters.

# Anne Cameron

# A Bear Story

I was looking for the honeytree
following the scent on the night air
knowing the stingers would be sleepy
in the cool blackness

There was a woman
naked in the moonlight
her skin gleamed pale
her eyes glittered like stars
she lay on the moss and grass
one hand on her belly
the other beneath her head
and when she saw me
she was unafraid

I wanted to walk lightly
I wanted to dance gracefully
I wished
so much
and she waited.
She was unafraid so I was, too,
and I lumbered close, sniffed carefully,
her neck, her underarm, her belly.
More fragrant than blossoms, tarter than berries,
filling my nostrils, making my head swim
and my belly grow tight and hot.
She parted her thighs and smiled
and I found honey without stingers
She gripped my ruff with her fingers
and arched against me, crooning,
crooning deep in her throat, eyes closed,
breath ragged, and we were there
until the sun was high in the sky.

## Florinda Colavin

# Desire

seduced by the creased lines of your palm
messages pumped to every cell
we were
bears
in a rage of spring heat

now
your odor
swarms about my head
dirty socks
stink to the ceiling
you leave a dark ring

i am fettered
with yearning
the bloodshot eye
flashing against my skin

your ass is fine
soft as baby hair at the nape of the neck

slip in once more
take the socks off me
we'll steam
into sunlight

i want
not
to want
to ache no more

# Eva Shaderowfsky

## What Will We Do About Angus?

"What will we do about Angus?" John said.

"I really don't know and don't really care." Louise sighed wearily.

Angus earned stud fees. He was a good bull and an excellent stud. It worked every time. He climbed on the cow's back, inserted his enormous penis, and that was it. Now that they were planning to separate, neither of them wanted to keep the farmhouse. Both were writers and had decided that the country was not a place to live alone. She was going to take a job as an editorial assistant in the city. He would teach and had already found a position as an adjunct, also in the city. The city would be large enough for them both, they agreed. They had a buyer for the house and its five acres. The man who was going to buy it owned the hardware store in town. He lived above it with his wife and three little kids, and was happy to buy the house and all the land that came with it so very reasonably. But he didn't want Angus.

John went outside and stood by the corral in which Angus was kept. The bull snorted, pawed the ground, and ran toward him. His fur was shiny, black, and thick. Altogether he was a solid creature—broad across the chest, the haunches, the back. John reached out to touch the wide space between his eyes. The animal allowed the touch for a moment, then whirled and charged to the other side of the enclosure. John started to call people—anyone he could think of—to try to find a buyer for Angus. He called the vet, the feed store, and all the farmers whose cows had been serviced by Angus. No one wanted him. "You know, it would help, Louise, if you tried a little." "Tried! I did try. That's why we're leaving each other. I tried and you didn't!" Her eyes bulged when she was angry. "I didn't mean our marriage. I mean Angus. What are we going to do about Angus?"

"That's your problem, thank God, not mine. And it really will be all yours Friday. I'm leaving at ten to catch the ten forty-five to the city." "How're you going to get to the station?" "You'll drive me, of course." He said nothing. He noticed her chin mole. He used to kiss it and say it was a spot of beauty. Well, now what? Put an ad in the paper. It would be clever, like YOU CAN TRUCK IT, AND ANGUS WILL— Nobody would print that. How about a limerick? THERE WAS ONCE A STUD NAME OF ANGUS. WHOSE AFFAIRS WITH THE WERE MOST . . . Nothing rhymes with Angus. Also too many words, too expensive. FOR SALE. MUST SELL CHEAP. He'd call the paper first thing in the morning.

It was getting dark when he went out into the cool dusk, hands in his pockets. He took a deep breath. It smelled good, of country air, and of Angus. She always complained when the wind came from the west. It brought Angus's smell right into the kitchen. Now, the bull stood on a knoll, silhouetted against the fading light. He was impressive! To watch Angus with a cow was exciting, especially at first. The best night they had together was after the first time he was used for stud. The cow's owner, an old farmer who was chewing on a piece of grass, kept up a running commentary during the whole procedure. Louise could barely keep from laughing every time the farmer said something. "Looks like he's gointa be able to get it in. She's standing nice and still for him, ain't she? Flora's one good cow, she is. Wisht I could say the same for Janet. She's my wife, you know. Lookee there! He's really puttin' it to her!" Then the old man cackled gleefully and spat to one side. That night, Louise wanted him to take her from the back. John thought of Angus with the cow. He felt that his penis was larger now than it had ever been. Louise cried out, "Harder. Harder!" When he came, he stayed erect. She marvelled at him. "Ooh, how big you are! It's still big! Didn't you come? I know you came. You want to do it again?" And they did. Four times that night. The next morning, he brought her breakfast in bed. After breakfast, he wanted to do it again. But Louise never dawdled, not even for a second cup of coffee on Sunday morning. She gave him a brisk kiss, and said, "Not now. I've got too many things to do."

He bought Angus shortly after they got married and moved in to the farmhouse. She was frightened of him at first, but more than that, she was furious with John for having spent so much money without consulting her. He apologized to her, saying that he had lived alone for too many years and that he'd have to get used to asking her advice, especially when it came to spending so much money. "Which we can't afford," he added. He helped her clear the table and even offered to wash the pots and pans. She said, no, she'd do it herself. While she was at the sink, he stood behind her, his arms around her waist. She allowed his touch, but he knew he had to be careful not to touch her breasts, for that familiarity would anger her now. "Okay," she said, "why did you buy that animal?" She moved out of his arms, dried her hands, hung up her apron, and faced him, waiting. "Well," said he, thinking of the dust kicked up when the bull turned suddenly, of his thick coat of coarse, black hair, of the sound his hooves made when he charged from one side of the corral to the other. "Well?" he said. "I, uh, I thought it would be good to have a farm animal at a farm. We have a farm now, so I thought we needed a farm animal," he said, smiling crookedly, and opening his blue eyes wide behind his glasses. "We *don't* have a farm! We have a farmhouse and a few acres. I, for one, do *not* want chickens and pigs, and I certainly don't want a bull! Of all the crazy . . ." "Now, wait, Louise, just listen to me," he interrupted her, feeling the excitement of his sudden inspiration build. "He won't cost us anything, because—now, just listen to this!— because we're going to use him for stud." "Stud?" "Yes. He's going to fuck all the cows who need to get fucked. Not only that, but we'll get paid for his services. Great, isn't it?" He beamed at her triumphantly. "You mean, people pay to have their cows studded?" "Serviced, not studded. Yes, they do. They pay a lot." She sat down at the kitchen table and was silent for a while. "We'll earn money?" "Yes, lots of it!" They had been living on free-lance work that took up most of their time. The thought of having more time in which to do her own work was very tempting.

As it turned out, they earned just a little more than what it cost to keep him. Although Louise seemed to enjoy watching every time that Angus serviced a cow, she complained to John about the bull's smell, especially when it rained. Also its stamping and snorting noises were bothersome. Altogether, she said, he was a nuisance and a terrible distraction. Then one day, she said that the bull had started to look at her in a peculiar way. She was afraid to leave the house, she said, whenever John went to town without her or left the farm to take his long walks. "Why are you afraid of Angus?" "That bull will get loose, that's why!" "Aw, no, Louise. I check that

fence every day. Every day! You've seen me. There's nothing to worry about." "Well, that bull could jump out if he
really wanted to." John looked out of the window over the
sink. I guess, he thought, if you see him on the knoll which
is high up, maybe it does look like he can jump out. But he
can't. As soon as he gets to the fence, anyone can see he
can't jump it. It's too high! Out loud, he said, "Louise, I
assure you he can't get loose. There's no way. Just don't
worry about it." But she continued to complain to him
about the look in the bull's eyes, until John lost patience
with her. He yelled. "Are you crazy!? What the hell are you
talking about? What do you think that look means, anyway?" "I don't know," she said, shrugging her shoulders
and looking down. "You think something about it, so for
chrissake, tell me!" She hesitated, looked down at her hands
in her lap and said, "I think the bull's got his eye on me."
"What's that supposed to mean?" But John knew what she
meant.

She sat before him, hands demurely clasped in her lap.
"John, I get scared when I'm alone with him. I walk out of
the house and he comes up to the fence and snorts and
then looks at me with those eyes. It gives me the shivers. He
doesn't act that way when you're around. Only when he's
alone with me." "Oh, come on, Louise. He acts that way all
the time. You're just seeing things, that's all. Maybe it would
be good for you to get out a little more. You're in the house
too much. You could even come with me." Which is what
she did.

They were together constantly. When he took his daily
two-hour walk, she went along. After half an hour, Louise
complained of sore feet, a pain in her lower back, and a
pounding headache. "You need good walking shoes." They
ordered a pair of walking shoes through the L. L. Bean
catalogue. And hiking socks. After she wore them in the
house for several days to break them in, they took another
walk. This time, she seemed to enjoy it. For forty-five minutes. Then she complained of increasing pain in her right
foot. When she took off her shoes, her right foot was
swollen. She was soaking it when he said, "Listen, Louise,
the walks aren't so good for you. Why don't you take the car
into town and do some shopping while I take my walks?" "I
don't *want* to go into town. There's nothing to do there. I
want to stay here and write. We moved here so we could have
some quiet for writing, didn't we?" What was he supposed
to say? He had considered it a sacrifice to take her along on

his walks. He needed that time to himself in order to think. As a matter of fact, he had been unable to write since that day that she told him about the look she saw in Angus's eyes.

She was with him constantly. Before, she wrote at the typewriter, which was set up on the dining-room table. He worked in longhand, sitting in an easy chair, in the spare bedroom. But now, she moved her typewriter to the small desk they kept in their bedroom, directly across from the spare bedroom. With the doors left open, they could see each other. Their rule not to disturb each other during worktime was not actually broken, but the typewriter, erratic and loud, made it difficult for him to concentrate. He closed his door one day after carefully explaining that he really needed just a little more privacy. But the room was small and with the door closed, he was uncomfortable. Also, the image of her eyes burning into the wood from the other side tormented him. "John?" she said softly from the other side of the door. "Yes?" "I brought you some tea, but I can't open the door, because I'm holding a tray." He put aside his pad and pen, and with a deep sigh, got up and opened the door. She had a forced grin on her face. Cheerily, she said, "Here we are! Isn't this nice?" She put the tray down on the bureau. "Mind if I join you in a cup of tea?" "Aw, Louise, you make me feel awful! I *do* mind. I haven't been able to write for weeks, because you're always with me. You've *got* to leave me alone for at least a couple of hours every day. Have you done any work at all?" She sat down on the bed and started to cry. "No. Not really. I don't know what's happening to me. Maybe it's this place. Maybe we should live somewhere else." "I thought you said it was Angus that was bothering you. Now it's the whole place!" She sat down next to him and took his hand. "It *is* Angus. If we got rid of him, I think I'd be fine again." He sighed deeply. "No, I don't think so. I think you just have to try to stop thinking about the bull. Put your mind to it. You were always such a strong person. You can do it if you want to." "I don't know. . . ." "Sure you do. You've just let this thing get the better of you, that's all. Now, let's have our tea and then I'm going to try to write for a couple of hours. You close your door, too." She did. He heard it close. But he couldn't write. He sat there looking at the closed door until he couldn't stand the stuffy air in the room. He opened it. Almost simultaneously, as if she'd been standing behind it, she opened her door. She looked pale and tired. "Oh!" she

said in that cheery voice. "You going to the bathroom, too?"
He didn't believe her. Her chin was red, in blotches. She had
been picking at her face and squeezing blackheads—not
writing. This was getting impossible. He knew that she was
trying to stay away from him during his work times. He also
knew that she was suffering. He could see it. At night, she
clung to him. He felt desire for her only on the nights after
Angus had performed. Then he always did it from the
back. He found he could not maintain an erection from the
front. He could no longer look at her.

Then came the day when she said that she was thinking
of leaving, that he should come with her. She wanted to
move back to the city—with him or without him. He was
relieved. Moving back to the city had been in his thoughts
recently. But when she said she'd go even if he didn't want
to, he understood clearly what he wanted. He told her he'd
go to the city, too, but without her. She was surprised, clung
to him and cried. He patted her back and felt her bony
shoulder blades. She smelled of stale sweat. The washing
machine is in the basement, he thought. I wonder if she's
been able to go down there to do a wash recently. He gently
disengaged himself when her crying had subsided. They
talked about their plans. She agreed that probably it would
be best if they were to separate, at least temporarily.

During the next few days, he saw that Louise was improv-
ing. She was bustling around, packing and cleaning, and he
even heard her humming. Her typewriter stood in its case
by the front door with the growing pile of cartons. When he
spoke to her, she answered "What?" turning her head vaguely
in his direction, not taking her eyes from what she was
doing. He was intruding, he felt. He began to wonder about
his decision to live without her. She was looking a lot better.
On Tuesday evening, she announced that she was all packed.
That night, she made a very good dinner. It was a beef stew
in wine sauce. Beef! How could I forget? he thought. "Louise!" he said. She looked up. "What?" "What will we do
about Angus?"

# Deena Metzger

# Ovation

Yesterday the blood-lined slit of the antelope
opened. He followed her logically
as the wolf follows his tongue to his balls
licking shit and mud from the winter fur.
Once I aspired to be a poet of knuckles and elbows,
pricks and nipples, brazen as a baboon with emblazoned ass.
If the grass parts, why not walk through it?
But my hands have the reluctant habit of fists,
nails growing through the palms.
I come to the trail with back pack, jerry cans of water,
too safe and therefore ill prepared,
neither on the road nor lost.
The passing of birds are the gusts of wind
and the lizard knows more than I do about the sun.
In the Sinai dunes the wind blew
the shape of a bed under my buttocks
then the menstrual dawn announced the rut
in trumpets of tiger lilies across the sky.
At dusk, the red sea is red
and when the sea parts it is to be entered.
So my hair is silver! The gray wolf
licks his ass and dreams of the delicate
ellipsis of blood. It's the season everywhere.
Get down on your hands and knees.

## Clarinda Harriss Lott

# Wolf Man

In the full moon
his hard hands grow the softest fur
and his taut lips soften
from the pressure
of the unfamiliar fangs
and he comes to you   comes to you
where you lie waiting
in your old-fashioned nightgown
shivering on your back
in the white bed of your girlhood.
There he grips the back of your neck
in his mouth   turns you over gently
warms your breasts in his silky forepaws
slipped under your body
and with his muzzle burrowed
in the night-chilled hair at your nape
his groinfur stroking your haunches
he mounts you   enters you
rocks you to the rhythm of his wolfdance
till you howl like a bitch
and the moon bursts.

# Maxine Kumin

# After Love

Afterwards, the compromise.
Bodies resume their boundaries.

These legs, for instance, mine.
Your arms take you back in.

Spoons of our fingers, lips
admit their ownership.

The bedding yawns, a door
blows aimlessly ajar

and overhead, a plane
singsongs coming down.

Nothing is changed, except
there was a moment when

the wolf, the mongering wolf
who stands outside the self

lay lightly down, and slept.

# Deborah Abbott

# This Body I Love

I am standing in the shower, in the large common shower, after seventy-two laps in the public pool. The water scalds my skin after the cool night air. I peel my suit down; stubborn over breasts and bottom, it suddenly slaps the tile at my feet. I step out and begin soaping, rubbing the almond-scented liquid over my shoulders, my arms. I am proud of these arms, growing broad after three weeks of swimming. They have propelled me through a mile of water tonight, arcing and scooping and pulling at the tremendous weight, and still they are not tired.

I raise my arms by turn and make a great lather in the hollows, in the thick, black ovals of hair. This hair that gathers the scent of me, blots it outward like a wick, and announces to my friends in the heat of day. I think—it's been ten years since I've stopped shaving it, since the pits of my arms prickled with insistent hairs, since blood beaded at the surface and clotted against my shirt. Ten years now of this hair, tangled as the twigs of a nest. Hold up my arms and small birds fly.

Oh, and then lovely, left arm still raised, suds careen down the slope of breast, heap on my nipple like cream on warm pie, then edge over, splatting the tile. Such fondness I have for these breasts, such pleasure they have known. Babies have choked on the milk of them, lovers have been finely sprayed and I, too, have tasted and touched. My breasts are those of a woman who has lived long and well. I call them lazy breasts now. They have done their work and lie on my chest like fruit upon the ground.

Now lower, soapy hands on my belly. Belly remembers those babies that rose from beneath until the skin was firm and resonant as a drum. Belly rounds, nostalgic. Fleshy, it makes a cushion for the cheek of a child.

Oh, then down, down, into the other nest, over Venus'

98

gentle mound. In this great tiled room there are four high spigots and a low one as well. I smile, remembering my young son discovering the one low-set in the corner. "Oh, they make one for kids," he exclaimed, his naked body delighting in its spray. "And for women in wheelchairs," I added, aloud. To myself I remember thinking "For women's genitals as well." I wanted to slide the soap between my folds then, to part my lips and let the water hum over them until they broke into song, but I reminded myself this was a shared space and mine a private tune. This time I rinse for half a minute, the fantasy as sweet as before. My fingers release and my labia settle together like petals of moonvine into the dark.

I lean over. My legs are long, one longer than the other. There is no symmetry in my legs, and, even after thirty years, this sometimes disturbs. After all, dutiful daughter that I was, I learned to part my hair precisely down the middle, with neither more nor less falling to either side. I cannot talk of my legs as one talks of eyes or ears or arms, usual pairs of these. I have always needed to buy two pairs of shoes, in different sizes, in order to have a single set that fit. My legs do not match. They will not match. They have not matched since a virus crept along my spine, consuming synapses as an insect chews its course along the nerve of a leaf.

My left hand grips the steel bar, steadies me, while my other squirts soap onto my great left thigh. "Thunder thigh" a lover called it once, as I wrapped it, vinelike, around a belly in the heat of love. This leg is thick with muscle. The Balancer. The Protector. The one that anticipates, compensates, takes the stairs, takes off in the pool, churning water behind like the wake of a whale. I hold on to the bar with both hands and lean back. The soap flows down, making rivulets through the forest of hair on my thighs, bubbling down my calf, over my toes, and onto the tile. It swirls round the drain and is loudly sucked down.

Now to my other. I stroke this slender limb, along the pale sutures whose indelible ribbons mark times the skin has been incised and peeled open, the bones broken and rearranged, the flesh stitched shut and left to mend beneath a wrapping of plaster. I am tender with this leg, forgiving, soaping it as I did a friend, fragile in her dying hours. I lift it a little, reaching the undercurve of foot.

I have never known how to name it. To make reference without causing further harm. The Small One? The Weak

One? The one that bows like a sapling in a climate of winds? I am a writer found inarticulate in the naming of a body that will not conform. That will not conform to the body of words a language holds. Perhaps the hands could make a sign that tells.

I turn and fill my mouth with water, spitting some, swallowing the rest. I wet my face, my hair. I am wet all over, warm and clean. I reach for shampoo. I make a lather in my hands, then pass it to my head, fingers massaging my scalp.

Two young women have entered the shower. They stand along the opposite wall, talking while they wash, all the while with their eyes closed. The force of their showers sends a cold wave of water over me. I shiver; my flesh puckers against the cold. For a moment I falter; then I catch the bar and hold fast.

I am not ashamed of looking. These women's bodies compel me. I watch them as though I were in a museum studying sculpture, as though I were eying shiny photos in a magazine. Perhaps these bodies are well-polished stone and mine the only blood-warmed flesh. Perhaps mine is the image fixed in the frame of a camera and theirs the flesh that is real.

I am not certain whether the water warms or my body accepts the water's chill, but finally my nipples lose their tension, the goose bumps leave my arms. This shower is like an enormous colander in which we all are contained and rinsed clean. And I am the ripened piece, irregular in form, yellow and softened and sweet. It is common knowledge that theirs, too, will ready with time.

# Lucille Clifton

# Homage to My Hips

these hips are big hips.
they need space to
move around in.
they don't fit into little
petty places. these hips
are free hips.
they don't like to be held back.
these hips have never been enslaved,
they go where they want to go
they do what they want to do.
these hips are mighty hips.
i have known them
to put a spell on a man and
spin him like a top!

# Maude Meehan

# On Second Thought

Last night's warm inspiration
write an erotic poem
So I sit here
cold early morning light
hard chair

Your body, familiar as my own
passes the window
working the garden
funky in sweaty
earth stained garb
old flop-brimmed hat

You are no help
conjure no visions
of flame-tongued nights
mad paroxysms of lust
or sutrian delights

Right now a second cup of coffee
a ripe and succulent peach
tempt me to leave this task
luring my senses with a pull
stronger than your proximity

On second thought
this is all that need be said
If you came in, touched,
took me to our bed
my breasts would swell
my nipples rise as they do now

\*     \*     \*

The hell with peaches
there is sweeter juice
let someone else write poems
Come in
there's better planting to be done

# Margaret Atwood

# Late August

This is the plum season, the nights
blue and distended, the moon
hazed, this is the season of peaches

with their lush lobed bulbs
that glow in the dusk, apples
that drop and rot
sweetly, their brown skins veined as glands

No more the shrill voices
that cried Need Need
from the cold pond, bladed
and urgent as new grass

Now it is the crickets
that say Ripe Ripe
slurred in the darkness while the plums

dripping on the lawn outside
our window, burst
with a sound like thick syrup
muffled and slow

The air is still
warm, flesh moves over
flesh, there is no
hurry

# Louise Thornton

# Careless Love

When the alarm jangled at five in the morning, Josie slid
her legs over the side of the bed and reached across to the
old wind-up clock clattering on the dresser. She turned it
off and then sat heavily on the side of the bed. The air was
biting cold in the unheated room, but she was drenched
with sweat. A wave of heat even stronger than the surges
she had experienced throughout the night began at her
neck and moved down over her body. The fine film of
moisture that had beaded over her skin pooled into large
drops.

As she stood up she caught a glimpse of herself in the
dresser mirror—dark, curly hair with threads of gray framing a small, round face, large breasts hanging full and
round, a great mound of stomach, wide hips riding each
side of her like wings folding into the soft nest of dark hair.
You've given me so much pleasure, she thought as she
stood gazing at her body. And now she had Robert who
trailed his tongue along the inside of her arms until she was
half wild with desire. But these hot flashes! She would be
glad when they stopped. She reached for her underpants and
bra and then her uniform. She had no use for housecoats.
They were for sick people.

She walked quickly through the living room along the
path she had left clear between piles of old newspapers,
clothes setting in plastic laundry baskets, and the faded,
upholstered couches and chairs she last vacuumed two years
ago. While her father and husband were still alive she kept
the house reasonably clean for them, dusting all of the glass
birds that had belonged to her mother, whom she could no
more remember than her grandmother buried in another
country. Her mother had died when she was four; she was
all her father had, once her brothers and sisters had married and moved away. She kept house for him even after

she married Joseph who moved in with them as if he were
the bride. Now her father had been dead for fifteen years
and Joseph for five.

When she came into the kitchen she saw the two teacups
still sitting on the table and smiled. The minister had been
to see her again last night. He was young with dark hair and
dark eyes, tall. Jesus, it would feel good to kiss him, she
thought every time she saw him. As they had sat drinking
tea the evening before, he had put his arm around her
shoulder and said, "You know, we miss you on Sundays,
Josie."

"Oh . . . do you?" she had answered. "I know I should
come. There's no excuse." How could she have told him
that every time she moved down the long, quiet aisle and sat
through the solemn service she felt as if she were attending
a funeral. "It's nice of you to be so concerned about me,"
she had said, looking into his eyes and refraining from
reaching out and touching his lips. "Do you care this much
about all your parishioners?"

"You're a very attractive woman, Josie," he had answered,
beginning to run his fingers along the bare skin on her
upper arm. In response she had eased herself into his
shoulder until tension hung in the air like damp heat. Then
she had caught herself. He was a minister with a wife and
two kids and if he didn't have enough sense to remember
this she would have to. She had whisked him out the door
with the excuse of having to get up early and carried his
fragrance with her into bed.

Now she bent to light the kerosene stove in the middle of
the floor. The flame was slow in staying lit, so she turned
up the fuel lever. The stove whooshed into flame just as the
three kittens who lived inside the old coal box next to the
stove crept near. They leaped back, flying in three different
directions. "Oh," she laughed, "poor kitties. Did you get
scared?" The smallest of the three eyed her suspiciously
from under the dish cupboard. When the kitten crawled
out and began to approach the heater again she plucked it
up with one hand, opened the top of her uniform, and
placed it between her breasts. Repeatedly she moved her
hand over the kitten's back, her fingers lingering over the
silken fur. A high-pitched twittering sound came from her
throat, and she rocked back and forth, pressing the kitten
ever closer.

Late one afternoon during the spring after her mother
died she had escaped from her brothers' and sisters' ever

watchful eyes and had crept down to the chicken house where she looked at the baby chicks for a long time, trying to decide which one to hold. Finally she had settled on the one peeping louder than all the others. She held the soft down, colored like fresh butter, against her cheek, but somehow this was not close enough; she wanted the chick inside her. She opened her mouth as wide as she could and put the chick on her tongue. It moved slightly, tickling the sides of her throat, and then was still. Closing her eyes, she breathed slowly, evenly, for several minutes. Then she carefully put the chick back under the brooder lights and went into the house.

Now she let the kitten go, giving it one final squeeze, and got up to make herself coffee. A half hour later she went out the back door, traveled the path between the forest of silver ash trees she had allowed to take over her father's garden, crossed a short, empty stretch of lawn, and opened the back door to the nursing home where she was in charge of the laundry.

After she entered Robert's room she quickly closed the door behind her and went to his bed. He had told her he was sixty-five, but he looked closer to seventy-five. Thin gray hair fell over his pale, deeply lined forehead, and his eyes looked watery without his glasses. "Hello, sweetie," she said. "Where's your roommate?"

"Oh, he's in the bathroom. You know him. He'll be in there forever! Did anyone see you come in here? I don't want you to get in trouble again. What if Mrs. Stevens fires you?"

"I can't help it if I come to work here and the first thing I see is this tall, handsome man. Besides, no one saw me." She bent over and kissed him long and full on the lips. Then in one quick movement she slid her hand into his pajama bottoms and gently grabbed his penis.

"Josie!" he whispered. "What if someone comes?"

She gave his penis a squeeze and then drew back to look at him. Her eyes narrowed into slits, the dark irises sparkling in sharp glitters, and she threw back her head and laughed. "Wouldn't that be something?" She glanced at the clock. "I have to go." Quietly she walked to the door, opened it slowly, and looked in both directions. "See you later," she whispered and slipped into the hall.

When she rounded the corner she came face to face with Mrs. Stevens walking down the hallway. Before Josie could think of an excuse for being near Robert's room so early in the day Mrs. Stevens said, "Josie, I'm afraid I need to have a little talk with you. . . . I like you and you do a very good job here but . . . well, you seem to be overly fond of one of our residents, Robert. And . . . well . . . your sister and brother, Tina and Peter, were here last night to see Minnie and we got to talking and we agreed . . ." Mrs. Stevens stopped talking and looked down the hallway as if she would find the words she needed to say written on the dull green walls.

Josie held her breath and her heartbeat quickened. She could not afford to lose this job. She had to support herself, and when other possibilities for employment flashed into her mind all she saw was the old, stale restaurant on Main Street where she had once worked as a waitress. She shuddered involuntarily.

Mrs. Stevens took a breath and continued. "You know how people talk in this town, and I do have to keep the reputation of this place in mind. So I'd appreciate it if you'd remember that Robert is a resident here and you're an employee."

Josie forced a laugh. "I think I can remember that."

"I knew you'd understand." She patted Josie on the shoulder. "See you later." What I understand, Josie thought as she marched down the hall, is that we're both human beings and what I do on my own time is none of anyone's business!

All morning she worked furiously in the laundry room, taking out her anger on thirty-five pairs of sheets, thirty-five towels, ten pairs of pajamas, twenty-five nightgowns, and a large assortment of shirts, trousers, dresses, and sweaters. By noon she was exhausted, but she looked with pride on the folded piles of laundry. She liked knowing that the residents would have fresh, clean clothing because of her hard work.

During her lunch break she stopped at the dining room to see Minnie, a second cousin on her father's side, who had been in the home since her husband died ten years ago. "How are you?" she asked, putting her arm around Minnie's frail shoulders.

"Oh, I'm going home tomorrow. My husband is coming to get me."

"But we would all miss you, Minnie!" Josie smiled at her broadly, her eyes shining. "Don't you want to stay with us?"

Minnie smiled back, her head constantly moving from side to side, and took Josie's hand. "How is Joseph? My, he's a little man! He's well, I hope?"

"Joseph died five years ago now. Remember?"

Minnie looked at her and then turned away quickly, but in the instant Josie had seen the fear in her eyes. "Oh, but I bet you never heard! How could you remember that Joseph died if no one ever told you?"

Minnie's eyes came back to meet Josie's. "No, no one ever told me. So Joseph died. That's too bad." Tears began to run down her cheeks and plop onto her thin, dry hands.

"It's all right," Josie said softly, cradling both of Minnie's hands in hers. "He was sick for two years and some days he just moaned all day. He would ask for a hot water bottle and I would bring him that and ten minutes later he wanted a cup of tea and when I brought him that he wanted me to rub his forehead because he had a headache. He kept me busy all day. He's happier now and I'm glad. He was a good husband." The memory of him riding her great body like a little goat was suddenly vivid in her mind and she laughed aloud.

Minnie's eyes began to sparkle and she smiled as if she, too, could see Joseph bouncing up and down. "My husband's coming to get me tomorrow and I hope he takes me straight to the bedroom. Oh! I shouldn't have said that," she cried then, her pale face blushing. "You must think I'm terrible."

"If you're terrible, then I'm a hopeless sinner!" Josie laughed so loud the other patients in the dining room turned and smiled as if they, too, were happily lost in perdition.

When Josie came back into her house at three thirty in the afternoon she opened the door to the sweet, extraordinarily pleasing aroma of apple pie. "Hello!" she called from the doorway. "Where's my honey?"

Slowly, cautiously putting each foot in front of the other, Robert came into the kitchen from the living room. "Here you are!" she called. "Come and give me a big kiss!" He began to shuffle forward but when he was still several feet away she grabbed him and kissed him on his lips, forehead, neck, cheeks, and then again on his lips. He stood, swaying in her arms. "Did you miss me?" she asked again and again.

"Yes, of course. You know I did!"

"And you made me a pie!"

"Yes! Yes! I wasn't a chef for fifty years for nothing! I made some tea, too. Would you like some?"

She looked at the table where at one end two plates and clean, white napkins had been carefully set side by side, and

she smiled broadly, looking at him, eyes radiant, her entire
face glowing. She could not remember anyone in her life
who had shown such kindness to her. "Oh, sweetheart!" she
cried. "I'd love some."

Later she made dinner: fat Polish sausages coiling on the
plate, potatoes sliced thick and fried to a crispy brown,
fresh steamed carrots in a white cream sauce. "Don't give
me much—just a bite," Robert said as she began to fill his
plate. "I'm not very hungry."

"You say that every night!" She heaped his plate almost as
high as hers. If he sat toying with the potatoes she picked
up a slice of sausage and held it to his mouth. "Eat!" she
commanded. "You're too thin already." He cleaned his plate.

Then they sat talking for a long while. Late afternoon sun
slanted in from the windows to the north and west and then
darkness came, soft and thick like a snowfall. She lit one
cigarette after another, inhaled deeply, threw her head back,
and then focused again on his face. He asked how her work
had gone in the laundry room, how she felt about the abuse
uncovered in a nursing home in a neighboring county,
whether or not she felt it was fair that single people receiving Social Security benefits would lose some of them if they
married. "You're so smart," she would say from time to
time.

These daily conversations were as important to her as the
lovemaking that would come later. Joseph had never been
interested in anything besides her, his health, and his car.
Robert engaged her mind so deeply that sometimes, in
answering one of his questions, she was surprised to find
that she did feel strongly about an issue. "What do you see
in me?" she asked now. "You're a college graduate. I never
went to high school."

"Oh, Josie," he answered. "What difference does that
make? You're as smart as anybody I went to school with.
Smarter!"

As she leaned to kiss him she heard the sound of footsteps on the front porch. "I wonder who that is?" she asked.
The door opened and her oldest brother, Charles, came
into the room without either knocking on the door or waiting to be invited inside. "I'm on my way to Zenith. Just
thought I'd stop by," he said. "Got some tea? It must be
close to zero out there."

"I should hope I have some tea." She laughed halfheartedly
and went to the stove to put on the kettle. They sat for a
while talking about the weather and other trivialities. Charles

ignored Robert, addressing all of his comments to Josie, who from time to time reached out and squeezed Robert's hand or said, "Isn't that right, Robert?" He nodded, smiling, but said little. Finally he rose from the table and said he was stepping outside for some fresh air.

Immediately Charles began yelling. "I thought I told you to stop fooling around with him! You're making a damn fool of yourself! Don't you have any self-respect? You can't sleep around just because you don't have a husband anymore."

She glared at him, her eyes glinting like obsidian. "I don't sleep around!"

"You can't carry on with a patient at the nursing home. You work there, for God's sake! You finally have a decent job and you're about to carelessly throw it away for a sick, old bastard!"

"He's a resident. He's not sick. The only reason he's there is because he has nowhere else to go."

"Who would want him! He's got to be close to eighty."

"What difference does it make how old he is? You're just using that as an excuse. You never liked Joseph either. Don't think I didn't hear you and Pete making fun of him every time you came here. Why can't you just leave me alone?"

"You're a stupid fool! That's why! You know what Bill Thompson said to me yesterday? 'You wouldn't believe what goes on in your sister's house. She and that old coot.' And Ed Weiss told me after church on Sunday that he thought it was disgraceful that Robert comes over here every chance he gets. 'They don't fool me!' he said. He thinks you should be fired from the home."

"I do a good job there and Mrs. Stevens knows it. The rest of them can mind their own business."

"Your sisters don't even want to be seen with you. Pete, Jacob, and I think you're not much better than a slut."

Tears welled in her eyes but she blinked them back. She would not look at him again. He could sit there for another hour and she would not acknowledge his presence. He stood up and put on his hat and coat. "Pa's not here anymore. Someone has to talk some sense into you. I thought I'd try, but it's like trying to talk to a dumb cow. Just remember this. If you don't kick that senile creep out of this house once and for all, no one in the family will have anything to do with you." He closed the door with a bang and was gone.

Almost without a sound Robert came back into the kitchen through the back door, walked over to Josie, bent down beside her chair, and began stroking her face with the tips of his fingers. She closed her eyes and the tears she had been holding back began to fall. "It's all right," he whispered.

"How can he still do this to me? When I was a little girl he made me cry all the time. It makes me furious that he still can. Why can't everyone just leave us alone?"

"Maybe they're jealous." She looked into his eyes. He was smiling. "You are a damn beautiful woman."

"Am I?"

"Absolutely. And you love me. I have nothing. I'm old. Every day I get a little older. But you love me. And I love you. Wouldn't you be jealous if you were someone else and saw how happy we are together?"

She laughed and grabbed him around the waist. He held out his hand. "Shall we?" he whispered.

"Oh, yes!" she exclaimed as she arose. Carefully he led her to the bedroom. As soon as she had closed the door she took his face in both of her hands and looked into his eyes, her own shining with light, and kissed him on each cheek and then on the mouth.

Moving against his body she unbuttoned his shirt, slid it off his arms, and hung it over the back of the chair so it would not be wrinkled when he returned to the home. Then she undid his belt, slipped it off, draped it over the chair, and slowly eased down the zipper in his trousers. "I've missed you all day," she whispered. Sliding her small hand under the elastic of his shorts she cuddled his penis still soft and limp in her hand. "Can you love me tonight do you think?"

"Oh, I want to," he answered fervently. "I hope I can."

She flung her arms around him and pressed against him with all of her weight. For a moment he wavered, trying to support her, but then he fell backward, and the two of them collapsed together on the bed.

"Now I have you where I want you," she half growled and began biting his shoulders and neck, drawing back after a particularly hard bite to make sure she had not broken the skin. "I love you!" she said into his neck and into the tender hollow between his shoulder and breastbone. She followed the line of his collarbone with kisses, kissed his neck, moved along the curve of his jaw with more kisses and stopped at his mouth with one long, noisy, final smack. "Now," she said, "it's time to let me see all of you."

After he slipped off the tangled trousers twisted around his knees she reached over and placed them next to his shirt, pressing the crease back with her fingers. Then she yanked off her uniform, unhooked her bra and slipped it off, pushed her underpants over her hips, and threw everything into a heap on the floor. They slid under the soft, warm feather bed her mother had made sixty years ago and between the soft, flannel sheets where they lay side by side, his arm around her, her hand resting on his chest.

Slowly he began to caress her breasts, his long, delicate hands circling round and round one, taking the nipple between his fingers and plucking it and then circling the other. She sighed deeply. "That feels so good . . . I love it so when you touch me." His hand moved down over the expanse of her stomach, slid along the hill of her hip and slipped into the fold inside her thigh. One finger and then another strayed into the neighboring mass of moist hair, drew back into the fold and then advanced again into the dampness. "Don't stop!" she whispered as his hand rested briefly. "Even if I die right here and now, don't stop."

He ran his hand alongside her leg, along the hair growing thick and dark on her thighs, along the tender folds between them, and along the great sweep of her hip turned now toward him. He kissed one eyelid and then the other, tongued the line of her eyebrows and then a spot just behind her ears.

With a cry she abruptly heaved up and flung herself against him, kissing him on the mouth long and hard. "I want you!" she shouted into the room.

"I'm not quite ready, my love. Can you wait just a little while longer?"

"Ohhhhhhhh . . . . . . . ! Oh God! I don't know . . ." she moaned, falling back onto the bed. Then her fingers began caressing his penis in its bed of wrinkled skin and slowly it began to rise. "That's it," she crooned. "It's time to get up now. Come on, sleepy head. You can do it. Come on . . . That's a boy. Get up now . . ." For a long time she sang, all the while stroking with strong, firm fingers, and steadily his penis grew until it stood tall and solid and rippling under her fingertips. "Now!" he whispered.

She rolled on top of him and as he guided into her she began rocking, her hips pressing into him in strong undulations until their bodies moved together like a great sea lion coming again and again to the receiving shore. "Now we're riding!" she cried. "Jesus, we're riding . . . . ." She rode faster, her song now a tone ever rising in pitch, shooting up through the ceiling, up through the roof, and finally bursting into the light spaces between the silver rustling trees in her father's garden.

Later, as she lay beside him, quiet now, her hand caressing his cheek, she asked, "Do you love me?"

"Yes. I love you. You know I do!" He traced his hand over her eyebrows and delicately moved his fingers over her lips like a child feeling the texture of his mother's face. "I love you more than life itself." She sighed, moved in closer, and they slept.

An hour later she began walking him back to the nursing home along the path through the garden. The night was bitter cold and patches of ice glimmered in the moonlight. "Now, you be careful!" she half scolded as they left the back door. "I don't want you to fall." She went first and he followed behind her, holding fast to her hips, and slowly they waddled over the ice and over the thin coating of snow. When they reached the door she drew him to her. "I'll never let you go!" she said fiercely. Then she kissed him one last time and turned back to the path.

I should go to bed, she said to herself when she was back in her kitchen. Instead she put on water for tea and switched on the old cabinet radio sitting in a corner of the kitchen. After turning the knob back and forth she found her favorite country-western station. "Love, oh love, oh careless love," she hummed along with Hank Williams. "Love, oh love, oh careless love. . . ." When the tea was done she took it to the table and sat down before the remaining half of the apple pie. She ate it leisurely, thinking of nothing but the sweet juice in her throat, the crumbly texture of the crust, the lush pulp of the apples on her tongue. When she was finished she drank the tea, turned off the lights, and went to bed.

Near twelve o'clock she awoke with a jolt. Flinging the covers from her she ran to the window, raised it as far as it would go, and lay down again, but she felt no cooler. A wave of heat ran along her backbone and down the length of her arms and legs and was quickly followed by another.

She got up again, walked quickly to the front door, yanked it open, and went out on the porch. As another spasm of heat walked over her, she looked to see if there were any headlights on the gravel road running by her house. No, not a one. In one quick movement she pulled her red rayon nightgown over her head and threw it to the ground. A band of cold began at the fine hairs along her neck, moved down over her nipples standing firm and lively, and continued along the curve of her breasts and then into the interior of her thighs. "Ahhhh . . ." she sighed as the cold caressed her buttocks and then began to circle her thick, strong legs. If the neighbors could see me now they'd really have something to talk about, she thought to herself.

Laughter began to rise up from her chest and weave around her breastbone. You can't make any noise, she said to herself, but the laughter heaved out of her throat of its own volition and pealed into the night. "You're crazy!" she shouted into the night. "You're a crazy woman!"

The melody from the old love song she had been humming earlier in the evening drifted again into her mind. "Love, oh love, oh careless love . . ." she sang quietly into the darkness and began to raise her arms above her head, swaying slightly from side to side, moving with the cold, with the bits of snow swirling in the wind, with the stars shining in the midnight sky, with the galaxies whirling all around her.

# Touching Fire

# Renée Ashley

# Rocking

I am draped sideways in the chair that is like a mouth, head tucked, body folded, bent in the middle like an elbow; my legs hang over the lacquered seawood arm, dangling like exposed roots. It is late, darker in here than I would ever imagine it could be with the stars and moon as lively as they are; only the fire, burnt low in the grate on the other side of the bed, gives shadows, forms that come and go, appear and then disappear again as I sit and rock with just the merest of sounds, laminated rocker against hard wood floor.

It is late and I haven't got a sleepy bone in my body, though Evan is wrapped tightly in sleep on the high brass bed in front of me, his rhythmical, light snore a wet part of the night sounds around me. This day, for Evan, has been longer than most, more difficult. He has been weary since early on. It would be too selfish not to let him sleep.

Yet there it is, sex building like an itch.

I can slide my leg out, slip it between the thick blue terrycloth edges of my robe, break open the cache with that single move, labia, like the pink-blushed lip of a shell.

Just the thought tips the balance, and the want of it washes through me like hot, wet sex itself.

I glance at Evan. He sleeps soundly; I won't wake him. He won't know that he has been left out; I won't tell him, though he must know that I can do this, scratch this particular itch without him. He must know it, yet, in all likelihood, he does not think about it. But the means is there, right there in my own hand; intuitive as hell, my fingers know their way, and, like a too-young lover, they are unabashedly eager though I am quite practiced now, now that these months without Evan have passed.

The first touch is good. Fingers probe, explore like sensitive antennae. The chair rolls forward like a wave on its smooth, splayed rockers as I reach, back again as I find. Equilibrium is all.

The first touch is good, yes, yet the entering is better, and the wetness of it triggers an unbelievable thirst, a thirst as immense as a craving for salt.

I drop my head back, and the chair finds its balance, stabler, upright, but that dull, starless ceiling suspended overhead is not what I want. In response, my eyes close like the eyes of a doll, but it is no good. And like the same doll thrown upright again the eyes fly open and I bring my head back down, forward on my neck; my fingers smooth flesh that is moist, like the inside of a cheek. Yet, I am not watching my fingers, but seeking out Evan, facing me on the bed, naked in this heat. It is Evan's sleeping form that I focus on, his curved arm, bent knees, genitals at rest, nestled like a rosebud at the very center of him. He sleeps like a child, but I could swear, as he shifts and brings his arm up to rest on his side, that he is responding, that he is aroused under my gaze, if only slightly now, and with this warmth of speculation my own need swells; urgency becomes a din behind my eyes that drowns out the rest of the night.

And my fingers do their magic, close to the bone, deeper, sink in and gorge on it while my hips rise like a tide, careful not to overturn the chair, not to make noise, not to wake Evan, and the wetness surrounds, the swollen flesh envelops, pulls down, nearly swallows in the heat, a lickerishness that bites its own parched lips.

And it builds. . . .

It builds and I throw myself up to it, arch like a strong fish, near now, and the chair below me trembles, and it builds, and I am carried by it, fingers, palm, elbow working, and I am stiff with it, taut, strung like a wire between the poles of myself, and when I come I buck, slam against my own strength, deeper and harder, exactly there, exactly right, and my eyes squeezed so tight that the pressure is nearly more than I can bear. . . .

And it is over, a wave, and then over again.

And when I bring my fingers back, draw them out across the mouth of the cache, they slide out, out and over, strike like a nerve that small nub that beats like my heart.

And when I can breathe and I roll back down like liquid, fold back down into the curve of my sweet, grotesque chair, Evan's eyes are on me, eyes greener in this dark than the grass in the moonlight.

And his invitation is mostly silent, thoroughly explicit, as he smooths the sheet in front of him. The sound of his hand on the linen is like a wash of breeze through leaves, and his smile and his welcome are wider than the dark itself. And he will wait; Evan will wait silently until I move, until I am able to move. He will wait and then, when I am willing to stand, I will go at my own speed to him and the night will close around us, will absorb us, and, when we have done, out the window I will choose a star and then I will certainly sleep, sleep like a water-smoothed stone, like agate in a stream.

# Deena Metzger

# Moon in Taurus

Across the barbed wire
the bull takes my hand,
it is lost in his mouth,
deeper, softer, warmer
than I dare think.
This is what it must be
to sink into a large woman
to submit to her ample thighs.
I am aware of boundaries,
his teeth, used to grass,
will not close on me,
he wants the salt,
wants me to sweat for him.

I have had to come east
to learn this animal
a real not mythic beast,
attended by dozens of heifers,
who seeks me out
under the horned full moon.
My hands stained with mulberries
come clean on that great tongue
slapping between my fingers,
his tail flits across his back,
his silken tassel quivers.

I have dreamed this animal
but not his gentleness
not that I would herd with him
that I would wish him
to nudge my flanks
his skin slouched over bones

a tent of a beast
not that he would drive me forward,
head down, hungry
through the night fields.

# Deborah Abbott

# The Coyotes

Nearly midnight. I am driving across town to your little house on the hillside, ignoring stop signs and all of the red and yellow lights. There is no use for them. There is no traffic at this hour. I hug the road to me like a body whose curves I have memorized in sleep.

Four days without you. Then moments ago, on the telephone, your voice low and sleepy, not exactly a whisper, but deep in your throat, saying "Djuna, would you come be with me now?"

"Yes," I answered. There were no other words. No breath.

I took my keys from the dresser, the one to your house on the ring beside mine. I put my bathrobe, deep purple, over my warm brown skin. I walked barefoot to the car.

I walk barefoot now up your three stone steps. I stand for a moment on your porch. I reach out and take the cool globe of your doorknob into my hand. I remember the first early morning I came here, my hand extending in the darkness toward a place I might take hold of, might touch. I remember my breath suspended, as it is now, until I heard the faint steady steps of your approach. Now I cradle the knob in my palm like a piece of fruit, a breast. I slip the brass key into the slot. It clicks. My wrist rolls over, exposed in the moonlight. Blood pulses there, its rhythm murmuring "Let me in. Let me in."

You are in bed on your belly, half-covered, illumined in the candlelight. Your sand-colored hair spreads like a collar over your bare shoulders. Your face is hidden in the pillow. Perhaps you are sleeping. Perhaps you are awake.

I move toward you. I stand beside your bed. The purple robe falls from my shoulders onto the floor. The air is cool. My nipples cluster like the poppies in your yard, curl into themselves, waiting for heat.

I reach out. With a single finger I slowly trace the length

124

of your spine. Vertebrae rise from the plain of your back like ridges forming at my touch. My finger travels down to your coccyx, to the place where your tail was once, before you came spilling out of the womb. This bone curves inward. I follow it down into the cleft between your cheeks. I let the soft pad of my finger rest over the swirl of your anus, your fuzz there like moss that grows where it is moist and dark. My finger remains, unmoving. My breath is shallow. I cannot hear your breath at all. Time passes without motion or sound.

And then slowly I feel you stirring. I feel you separate beneath my hand. You are spreading. You are lifting up onto your haunches. The first syllables take shape in your mouth. "Djuna," you say, "take me . . . like this."

You are a coyote in heat. Your scent has drawn me across the prairie, through the tall rye, past the cottonwoods, the stand of tamarisk. The moon is full. I stand on the butte watching you. Your yellow eyes are closed against the light. Your neck is arched backward as though you were in song. But you have grown quiet.

I find you waiting on a shelf of granite. Expectant. Alert. I approach you directly from behind. I put my muzzle against you, sniffing. The breath from my snout is warm. It covers that which you present: knot of anus, bulge of vulva. Moisture collects on the fur of your pubis like fog. I nudge you; my nostrils flare at your crotch. A growl forms in your throat, but you do not move.

My long tongue falls out of my muzzle. I begin lapping along your rise. You turn wildly, snarling and snapping. And then I pounce on you; my teeth sink into the thick mantle of fur at your throat. You whimper. Your forelegs collapse. You present to me. My teeth slowly release you. I lick at your vulva. I lick until I taste that which I have sought, that which directed me all of those miles. Your genitals are hanging, engorged. I feel my own, heavy with blood and the fluid of mating. I throw back my head and howl. You answer. For a moment you straighten. We stand there, our throats bared, crying into the night.

I am on you then and in you. My mouth takes you by the ruff. You struggle. You shake your head, trying to throw me off. Then you are still. I hear you panting. I see your breath forming clouds around your gaping muzzle. I am hunched over you. I enter again and again. Each time you yelp. You shudder against me. Each time I withdraw from you, my own organs contract. Their rhythm is like a heart-beat, quickening.

"Djuna," you say, "I want more of you. More." I am filling you with my fingers. You are full and wet. I am deeply in your anus. Most deeply there, but in your vagina as well. More of me there. Gliding into your wetness until I find the end of you. Circling there. The pressure of me each time drawing your breath in sharply. I move faster. You are rocking against me. Moaning.

You are suddenly still. You are completely receptive. There is no sound from you, only that of my fingers moving in you. Moving out.

Then your head is back. Your jaw falls open. You let out one long howl. Your hindlegs give way. My teeth loosen from your mantle and I fall upon you, trembling. A wetness pours out of me, pungent and hot; it flows over your vulva. You roll away from me, wriggling in the dirt. I expose my belly to you. You lunge at me, playful. You tug at my nipples until I leap and give chase. You streak along the length of granite, ducking in and out of the silver-green sage. You vault straight into the air and turn, dashing toward me.

Our shadows are long in the moonlight. Leaves of the aspen flutter against the wind. You beckon to me finally, cocking your head from side to side. I follow you to the thicket of willow that is your bed. You circle and settle yourself down. You lick at my muzzle. I curl around your buff-colored flank. We sleep.

# Nancy Redwine

# Lot's Wife

I lie on the beach remembering Lot's wife,
remembering the tongues of cows as I lay in a field
developing curves,
remembering the taste of my fingertips after draping them
through you.
I am a block of salt glittering in the sun
blinding cows and low-flying planes.
Broad pink and black tongues are drawn across my surface.
I am licking you clean,
sucking the salt
that frosts the tiny hairs on your chest.
I lick the slow formations from your chin
the lace from your neck.
Mingling so, we could name our own sea.
I once thought they were blocks of ice,
too stubborn and cold to melt, left out in the rain
so the cows had something to stare at.
I am melting in layers, you lick them away patiently
as if they were placentas.
I am remembering her clearly now, her head turned slightly
a last look at her burning home
her ear turning to the cries, familiar voices. Her eyes
suddenly full of light.
Salt is dripping from my body
tiny stalactites, thin crocheted strips
flapping against me as I roll toward you.
You are licking my body into a new shape.
I lie in a field of sheets, quenching your broad tongue.

# Jan Sturtevant

# Rain Tree

The ground on the island is so dry it cannot absorb this sudden rainfall. The hot air is thick with the smell and taste of dust, of dampness. We are alone. Only curtains separate our room from the others. We have entered unobserved, not knowing when the revelers might tire and return from the endless No Ruz celebrations. Through the open window the steady rainfall softens words to murmurs, to whispers.

You approach me slowly, palms out, barely touching my breasts. We hold ourselves apart, tongue-tips flicking. I inhale sharply and my breasts press into your hands. Leaning together, we exhale, sink into the heat surrounding us. I sway, eyes closed. You nudge inside my collar, nipping and licking down the slope of my breast. My fingers lace tighter at your waist—holding on for the familiar slide.

*I remember the nights you tapped on my window and I slipped out of my parents' house—a thin blanket around me—and met you in the garden under the Golden Rain Tree.*

I breathe again, open my eyes, hold you with my gaze. "Come here," I whisper, opening your mouth with my kisses, sucking your tongue in on top of mine. Our bodies press through cloth, our clothes slide off in heat, in dampness. Now we hurry. My hands slip over sweat-slicked skin—I cannot hold you. Rain sounds mix with the sound of our wet bodies slapping together. Your eyes squeeze shut—you are suddenly still. Our bodies listen: your thrusts turn to one strong pulse. It subsides and I pull you down. We rock each other, locked at hips, legs and arms tightly bound.

"Listen to the rain," you whisper. I pull away and hear instead a summer wind in the Golden Rain Tree.

# Dorianne Laux

## China

From behind he looks like a man
I once loved, that hangdog slouch
to his jeans, a sweater vest, his neck
thick veined as a horse cock, a halo
of chopped curls.

He orders coffee and searches
his pockets, first in front, then
from behind, a long finger sliding
into the slitted denim like that man
slipped his thumb into me one summer
as we lay after love, our freckled
bodies two plump starfish on the sheets.

Semen leaked and pooled in his palm
as he moved his thumb slowly,
not to excite me, just to affirm
he'd been there.

I have loved other men since, taken
them into my mouth like a warm vowel,
lain beneath them and watched their irises
float like small worlds in their open eyes.

But this man pressed his thumb
toward the tail of my spine
like he was entering
China, or a ripe papaya
so that now when I think of love,
I think of this, his thumb a wandering
stranger between my hips.

# Sharon Olds

## It

Sometimes we fit together like the creamy
speckled three-section body of the banana, that
joke fruit, as sex was a joke when we were kids,
and sometimes it is like a jagged blue comb of glass across
          my skin,
and sometimes you have me bent over as thick paper can be
folded, on the rug in the center of the room
far from the soft bed, my knuckles
pressed against the grit in the grain of the rug's
          braiding where they
laid the rags tight and sewed them together,
my ass in the air like a lily with a wound on it
and I feel you going down into me as
if my own tongue is your cock sticking
out of my mouth like a stamen, the making and
breaking of the world at the same moment,
and sometimes it is sweet as the children we had
thought were dead being brought to the shore in the
narrow boats, boatload after boatload.
Always I am stunned to remember it,
as if I have been to Saturn or the bottom of a trench in the
          sea floor, I
sit on my bed the next day with my mouth open and think
of it.

# Cathryn Alpert

# Where We Are Now

Now we are climbing the steep canyon, a cleft between walls of white oak and pine where concrete gives way to dense forest. Your hand resting on my knee, you break touch to shift gears, comb a stray hair from your forehead. The engine revs, sings a higher tune, as our car lunges forward like the sleek cat it was named after. Pushes up, into the thick of it, beyond the point where the road narrows like a river flowing backward.

Now we are passing the summer camp, its bright lights blinking through foliage like eyes through a keyhole. They watch us climb, snake our way up the steep mountain to our secret place at the end of the road, where signs on trees tell us what not to do: NO PARKING, nailed to the log on the left. On the right: NO TRESPASSING, stapled to a pine.

Now you are turning the car around, our headlights glinting off heavy chains that bar our entry further up the canyon. You park in the dirt at the side of the road, switch off engine and headlights, set the parking brake. Slowly, our eyes adjust to darkness, reveal a huge moon rising through tall timber, the pregnant belly of a new season upon us.

Now you are ripping at snaps and buttons, and I, at your zipper, and somehow we manage to both come undone, a tangle of introverted pantlegs and sleeves. You climb on top of me as we jockey for position around the hand brake. An unwelcome intruder, it jabs into my hip, cold and hard as the cock of a steel boar. I wince and rock my pelvis forward as you thrust into the cleft between my legs and mount me like the young buck you once were. No time for foreplay—we have to be quick and beastlike up here in the forest. I clutch at your bare thighs, you at my shoulders, and together we ride each other hard, the moon pulling you in and out of me like a tide.

And now, the sudden arc of headlights makes us freeze. We still our hearts, lie breathless as the lights sweep, ghost-like, through the trees and disappear behind a mountain. Quietly, we watch for their return, ready to leap like fright-ened stags at all but the faintest glimmer. We stalk the lights with our eyes, search thicket and glen. See only the skeletal limbs of ancient oaks; the moon, burgeoning, yellow sow.

And soon we are rising again, and falling, comfortable in our animal rhythm. I nuzzle your shoulder; you nip at my neck, run your tongue down over my joggling breast. We are reckless and oh, so naughty, my hip rocking against the hand brake, your bare butt mooning the moon. I reach up, slide open the sunshade. See crisp leaves dancing on harvest wind. NO FUCKING written into the stars.

And now we are reaching the high ground, climbing stealthily as our cat-car climbed the mountain; inching si-lently, as water up a well. Your pace quickens as we writhe in the darkness, straddle bucket seats not made for this kind of driving. I struggle beneath the weight of you, adjust hips and thighs, plant one foot against the steering wheel. Curse the priapismic hand brake.

And when you are deep in my center, like a great mouth I feel the whole of me open up to you, wide for your taking, wide enough to swallow the earth. And all that I am is the feel of you: the slap of your hips ramming my thighs, the tug of your mouth on my nipple, the thrust of your cock deep at my core. The heat from our bodies, rising. We muffle our cries, bite down hard on lips and tongues, leave noiseless tracks on slippery skin, careful not to wake the forest.

And now we are laughing, harder than the time before. The car shakes with our laughter, threatens to roll us, coupled and naked, down into the village. We hunt for Kleenex in the bottom of my purse—there is never enough Kleenex—and make do with the few balled-up wads we ferret among pen caps, emery boards, and snarls of hair. Dismounting me, you return to your seat and I, to mine, where we make a mess of ourselves cleaning up—we are laughing so hard—tossing slimy Kleenex on the backseat floor next to Gummi Bear wrappers and little metal cars. We tug at our tangled jumble of clothes. Struggle, wet, into rumpled jeans so we can go on to our movie, a poorly lit place where we will probably stick to the seats.

But first we must stop laughing. There is no more Klee-nex to wipe away our tears. We swipe at our faces with the sleeves of our shirts and still we laugh, the windshield fogged over, the air inside the car so stifling we gasp. We open windows wide, let in the breeze that soothes our lungs, dries streams of tears to our faces. The car fills with the loamy scent of earth and pine, flickers with the rustling of leaves in moonlight. And we hear voices: from the camp below, a chorus of children's laughter mingling with our own, ringing off tall pines, echoing down the canyon.

And now our laughter is fading to reflection. We lean back in our seats, watch fog evaporate from tinted glass. Below us, songs around a campfire. Above, the spotted branches of an old, arthritic oak. We are forty now—not young, but not yet sober. You reach for my knee; I, for your hand, and together we forget about our movie, content ourselves to watch, instead, the Little Bear tracking ageless circles around our northernmost star. A cool gust whistles up the canyon. Tree limbs dance their autumn waltz, rain silver leaves through open windows. And the moon, so full of our transgression, smiles. Seems frozen in that one moment between waxing and waning, when it appears most whole.

# Kathy Metcalfe

# Piñata

She wants him to take
her widowhood
That is why she is here
in this stable
watching him feed horses
watching him swing the big fork
tear the hay from the bale
toss it to the slobbering
velvet mouths
She smells dust and sweat
timothy and clover
She smells the stallion's urine
pouring in a hot stream
splashing on the earth floor
Between her legs she feels
a sort of whimper and is glad
when the man leans the fork
against the rough boards to
climb up beside her
He lays her down
fills her mouth with his tongue
only tiny vowels escape from her throat
She feels her back lengthen under him
each cartilage opening like a flower
on her spine
Under his heaviness
she fights to spread her legs
to crook her knees
point them toward the rafters
Her hands widen and close on his back
Her head rolls from side to side
She didn't know it would be like this

134

The dark ceramic night holding so many toys
In the early hours of morning
she abandons her grief
bursts like a piñata

# Audre Lorde

## Excerpt from Zami:
## A New Spelling of My Name

Gerri was young and Black and lived in Queens and had a powder-blue Ford that she nicknamed Bluefish. With her carefully waved hair and button-down shirts and gray-flannel slacks, she looked just this side of square, without being square at all, once you got to know her.

By Gerri's invitation and frequently by her wheels, Muriel and I had gone to parties on weekends in Brooklyn and Queens at different women's houses.

One of the women I had met at one of these parties was Kitty.

When I saw Kitty again one night years later in the Swing Rendezvous or the Pony Stable or the Page Three—that tour of second-string gay bars that I had taken to making alone that sad lonely spring of 1957—it was easy to recall the St. Alban's smell of green Queens summer-night and plastic couch covers and liquor and hair oil and women's bodies at the party where we had first met.

In that brick-faced frame house in Queens, the downstairs pine-paneled recreation room was alive and pulsing with loud music, good food, and beautiful Black women in all different combinations of dress.

There were whipcord summer suits with starch-shiny shirt collars open at the neck as a concession to the high summer heat, and white gabardine slacks with pleated fronts or slim ivy-league styling for the very slender. There were wheat-colored Cowden jeans, the fashion favorite that summer, with knife-edged creases, and even then, one or two back-buckled gray pants over well-chalked buckskin shoes. There were garrison belts galore, broad black leather belts with shiny thin buckles that originated in army-navy surplus stores, and oxford-styled shirts of the new, iron-free Dacron, with its stiff, see-through crispness. These shirts, short-sleeved and man-tailored, were tucked neatly into belted pants or

136

tight, skinny straight skirts. Only the one or two jersey knit shirts were allowed to fall freely outside.

Bermuda shorts, and their shorter cousins, jamaicas, were already making their appearance on the dyke-chic scene, the rules of which were every bit as cutthroat as the tyrannies of Seventh Avenue or Paris. These shorts were worn by butch and femme alike, and for this reason were slow to be incorporated into many fashionable gay-girl wardrobes, to keep the signals clear. Clothes were often the most important way of broadcasting one's chosen sexual role.

Here and there throughout the room the flash of brightly colored below-the-knee full shirts over low-necked tight bodices could be seen, along with tight sheath dresses and the shine of high thin heels next to bucks and sneakers and loafers.

Femmes wore their hair in tightly curled pageboy bobs, or piled high on their heads in sculptured bunches of curls, or in feather cuts framing their faces. That sweetly clean fragrance of beauty-parlor that hung over all Black women's gatherings in the fifties was present here also, adding its identifiable smell of hot comb and hair pomade to the other aromas in the room.

Butches wore their hair cut shorter, in a D.A. shaped to a point in the back, or a short pageboy, or sometimes in a tightly curled poodle that predated the natural afro. But this was a rarity, and I can only remember one other Black woman at that party besides me whose hair was not straightened, and she was an acquaintance of ours from the Lower East Side named Ida.

On a table behind the built-in bar stood opened bottles of gin, bourbon, Scotch, soda, and other various mixers. The bar itself was covered with little delicacies of all descriptions; chips and dips and little crackers and squares of bread laced with the usual dabs of egg-salad and sardine paste. There was also a platter of delicious fried chicken wings, and a pan of potato-and-egg salad dressed with vinegar. Bowls of olives and pickles surrounded the main dishes, with trays of red crab apples and little sweet onions on toothpicks.

But the centerpiece of the whole table was a huge platter of succulent and thinly sliced roast beef, set into an underpan of cracked ice. Upon the beige platter, each slice of rare meat had been lovingly laid out and individually folded up into a vulval pattern, with a tiny dab of mayonnaise at the crucial apex. The pink-brown folded meat around the pale cream-yellow dot formed suggestive sculptures that made a great hit with all the women present, and Pet, at whose house the party was being given and whose idea the meat sculptures were, smilingly acknowledged the many compliments on her platter with a long-necked graceful nod of her elegant dancer's head.

The room's particular mix of heat-smells and music gives way in my mind to the high-cheeked, dark young woman with the silky voice and appraising eyes (something about her mouth reminded me of Ann, the nurse I'd worked with when I'd first left home).

Perching on the edge of the low bench where I was sitting, Kitty absently wiped specks of lipstick from each corner of her mouth with the downward flick of a delicate forefinger.

"Audre . . . that's a nice name. What's it short for?"

My damp arm hairs bristled in the Ruth Brown music, and the heat. I could not stand anybody messing around with my name, not even with nicknames.

"Nothing. It's just Audre. What's Kitty short for?"

"Afrekete," she said, snapping her fingers in time to the rhythm of it and giving a long laugh. "That's me. The Black pussycat." She laughed again. "I like your hairdo. Are you a singer?"

"No." She continued to stare at me with her large direct eyes.

I was suddenly too embarrassed at not knowing what else to say to meet her calmly erotic gaze, so I stood up abruptly and said, in my best Laurel's-terse tone, "Let's dance."

Her face was broad and smooth under too-light makeup, but as we danced a foxtrot she started to sweat, and her skin took on a deep shiny richness. Kitty closed her eyes part way when she danced, and her one gold-rimmed front tooth flashed as she smiled and occasionally caught her lower lip in time to the music.

Her yellow poplin shirt, cut in the style of an Eisenhower jacket, had a zipper that was half open in the summer heat, showing collarbones that stood out like brown wings from her long neck. Garments with zippers were highly prized among the more liberal set of gay-girls, because these could be worn by butch or femme alike on certain occasions, without causing any adverse or troublesome comments. Kitty's narrow, well-pressed khaki skirt was topped by a black belt that matched my own except in its newness, and her natty trimness made me feel almost shabby in my well-worn riding pants.

I thought she was very pretty, and I wished I could dance with as much ease as she did, and as effortlessly. Her hair had been straightened into short feathery curls, and in that room of well-set marcels and D.A.'s and pageboys, it was the closest cut to my own.

Kitty smelled of soap and Jean Naté, and I kept thinking she was bigger than she actually was, because there was a comfortable smell about her that I always associated with large women. I caught another spicy, herblike odor, that I later identified as a combination of coconut oil and Yardley's lavender hair pomade. Her mouth was full, and her lipstick was dark and shiny, a new Max Factor shade called "Warpaint."

The next dance was a slow fish that suited me fine. I never knew whether to lead or to follow in most other dances, and even the efforts to decide which was which was as difficult for me as having to decide all the time the difference between left and right. Somehow that simple distinction had never become automatic for me, and all that deciding usually left me very little energy with which to enjoy the movement and the music.

But "fishing" was different. A forerunner of the later one-step, it was, in reality, your basic slow bump and grind. The low red lamp and the crowded St. Alban's parlor floor left us just enough room to hold each other frankly, arms around neck and waist, and the slow, intimate music moved our bodies much more than our feet.

That had been in St. Alban's, Queens, nearly two years before, when Muriel had seemed to be the certainty in my life. Now in the spring of this new year I had my own apartment all to myself again, but I was mourning. I avoided visiting pairs of friends, or inviting even numbers of people over to my house, because the happiness of couples, or their mere togetherness, hurt me too much in its absence from my own life, whose blankest hole was named Muriel. I had not been back to Queens, nor to any party, since Muriel and I had broken up, and the only people I saw outside of work and school were those friends who lived in the Village and who sought me out or whom I ran into at the bars. Most of them were white.

"Hey, girl, long time no see." Kitty spotted me first. We shook hands. The bar was not crowded, which meant it probably was the Page Three, which didn't fill up until after midnight. "Where's your girlfriend?"

I told her that Muriel and I weren't together any more. "Yeah? That's too bad. You-all were kinda cute together. But that's the way it goes. How long you been in the 'life'?"

I stared at Kitty without answering, trying to think of how to explain to her, that for me there was only one life—my own—however I chose to live it. But she seemed to take the words right out of my mouth.

"Not that it matters," she said speculatively, finishing the beer she had carried over to the end of the bar where I was sitting. "We don't have but one, anyway. At least this time around." She took my arm. "Come on, let's dance."

Kitty was still trim and fast-lined, but with an easier looseness about her smile and a lot less makeup. Without its camouflage, her chocolate skin and deep, sculptured mouth reminded me of a Benin bronze. Her hair was still straightened, but shorter, and her black Bermuda shorts and knee socks matched her astonishingly shiny black loafers. A black turtleneck pullover completed her sleek costume. Somehow, this time, my jeans did not feel shabby beside hers, only a variation upon some similar dress. Maybe it was because our belts still matched—broad, black, and brass-buckled.

We moved to the back room and danced to Frankie Lymon's "Goody, Goody," and then to a Belafonte calypso. Dancing with her this time, I felt who I was and where my body was going, and that feeling was more important to me than any lead or follow.

The room felt very warm even though it was only just spring, and Kitty and I smiled at each other as the number ended. We stood waiting for the next record to drop and the next dance to begin. It was a slow Sinatra. Our belt buckles kept getting in the way as we moved in close to the oiled music, and we slid them around to the side of our waists when no one was looking.

For the last few months since Muriel had moved out, my skin had felt cold and hard and essential, like thin frozen leather that was keeping the shape expected. That night on the dance floor of the Page Three as Kitty and I touched our bodies together in dancing, I could feel my carapace soften slowly and then finally melt, until I felt myself covered in a warm, almost forgotten, slip of anticipation, that ebbed and flowed at each contact of our moving bodies.

I could feel something slowly shift in her also, as if a taut string was becoming undone, and finally we didn't start back to the bar at all between dances, but just stood on the floor waiting for the next record, dancing only with each other. A little after midnight, in a silent and mutual decision, we split the Page together, walking blocks through the West Village to Hudson Street where her car was parked. She had invited me up to her house for a drink.

The sweat beneath my breasts from our dancing was turning cold in the sharpness of the night air as we crossed Sheridan Square. I paused to wave to the steadies through the plate-glass windows of Jim Atkins's on the corner of Christopher Street.

In her car, I tried not to think about what I was doing as we rode uptown almost in silence. There was an ache in the well beneath my stomach, spreading out and down between my legs like mercury. The smell of her warm body, mixed with the smell of feathery cologne and lavender pomade, anointed the car. My eyes rested on the sight of her coconut-spicy hands on the steering wheel, and the curve of her lashes as she attended the roadway. They made it easy for me to coast beneath her sporadic bursts of conversation with only an occasional friendly grunt.

"I haven't been downtown to the bars in a while, you know? It's funny. I don't know why I don't go downtown more often. But every once in a while, something tells me go and I go. I guess it must be different when you live around there all the time." She turned her gold-flecked smile upon me.

Crossing 59th Street, I had an acute moment of panic. Who was this woman? Suppose she really intended only to give me a drink that she had offered me as we left the Page? Suppose I had totally misunderstood the impact of her invitation, and would soon find myself stranded uptown at 3 A.M. on a Sunday morning, and did I even have enough change left in my jeans for carfare home? Had I put out enough food for the kittens? Was Flee coming over with her camera tomorrow morning, and would she feed the cats if I wasn't there? If I wasn't there.

If I wasn't there. The implication of that thought was so shaking it almost threw me out of the car.

I had had only enough money for one beer that night, so I knew I wasn't high, and reefer was only for special occasions. Part of me felt like a raging lioness, inflamed in desire. Even the words in my head seemed borrowed from a dime-store novel. But that part of me was drunk in the thighed nearness of this exciting unknown dark woman, who calmly moved us through upper Manhattan, with her patent-leather loafers and her camel's-hair swing coat and her easy talk, from time to time her gloved hand touching my denimed leg for emphasis.

Another piece of me felt bumbling, inept, and about four years old. I was the idiot playing at being a lover, who was going to be found out shortly and laughed at for my pretensions, as well as rejected out of hand.

Would it be possible—was it ever possible—for two women to share the fire we felt that night without entrapping or smothering each other? I longed for that as I longed for her body, doubting both, eager for both.

And how was it possible, that I should be dreaming the roll of this woman's sea into and around mine, when only a few short hours ago, and for so many months before, I had been mourning the loss of Muriel, so sure that I would continue being broken-hearted forever? And what then, if I had been mistaken?

If the knot in my groin would have gone away, I'd have jumped out of the car door at the very next traffic light. Or so I thought to myself.

We came out of the Park Drive at Seventh Avenue and 110th Street, and as quickly as the light changed on the now deserted avenue, Afrekete turned her broad-lipped, beautiful face to me, with no smile at all. Her great lidded, luminescent eyes looked directly and startlingly into mine. It was as if she had suddenly become another person, as if the wall of glass formed by my spectacles, and behind which I had become so used to hiding, had suddenly dissolved.

In an uninflected, almost formal voice that perfectly matched and thereby obliterated all my question marks, she asked, "Can you spend the night?"

And then it occurred to me that perhaps she might have been having the same questions about me that I had been having about her. I was left almost without breath by the combination of her delicacy and her directness—a combination that is still rare and precious.

For beyond the assurance that her question offered me—a declaration that this singing of my flesh, this attraction, was not all within my own head—beyond that assurance was a batch of delicate assumptions built into that simple phrase that reverberated in my poet's brain. It offered us both an out if necessary. If the answer to the question might, by any chance, have been no, then it's very syntax allowed for a reason of impossibility, rather than of choice—"I can't," rather than "I won't." The demands of another commit-

ment, an early job, a sick cat, etc., could be lived with more
easily than an out-and-out rejection.

Even the phrase "spending the night" was less a euphe-
mism for making love than it was an allowable space provided, in which one could move back or forth. If, perhaps, I
were to change my mind before the traffic light and decide
that no, I wasn't gay, after all, then a simpler companion-
ship was still available.

I steadied myself enough to say, in my very best Lower
East Side Casual voice, "I'd really like to," cursing myself
for the banal words, and wondering if she could smell my
nervousness and my desperate desire to be suave and debo-
nair, drowning in sheer desire.

We parked half-in and half-out of a bus stop on Manhattan Avenue and 113th Street, in Gennie's old neighborhood.

Something about Kitty made me feel like a roller coaster,
rocketing from idiot to goddess. By the time we had col-
lected her mail from her broken mailbox and then climbed
six flights of stairs up to her front door, I felt that there had
never been anything else my body had intended to do
more, than to reach inside of her coat and take Afrekete
into my arms, fitting her body into the curves of mine
tightly, her beige camel's-hair billowing around us both, and
her gloved hand still holding the door key.

In the faint light of the hallway, her lips moved like surf
upon the water's edge.

It was a one-and-a-half-room kitchenette apartment with
tall narrow windows in the narrow, high-ceilinged front
room. Across each window, there were built-in shelves at
different levels. From these shelves tossed and frothed,
hung and leaned and stood, pot after clay pot of green and
tousled large and small-leaved plants of all shapes and
conditions.

Later, I came to love the way in which the plants filtered
the southern-exposure sun through the room. Light hit the
opposite wall at a point about six inches above the thirty-
gallon fish tank that murmured softly, like a quiet jewel,
standing on its wrought-iron legs, glowing and mysterious.

Leisurely and swiftly, translucent rainbowed fish darted
back and forth through the lit water, perusing the glass
sides of the tank for morsels of food, and swimming in and
out of the marvelous world created by colored gravels and
stone tunnels and bridges that lined the floor of the tank.
Astride one of the bridges, her bent head observing the
little fish that swam in and out between her legs, stood a

little jointed brown doll, her smooth naked body washed by the bubbles rising up from the air unit located behind her.

Between the green plants and the glowing magical tank of exotic fish, lay a room the contents of which I can no longer separate in my mind. Except for the plaid-covered couch that opened up into a double bed that we set rocking as we loved that night into a bright Sunday morning, dappled with green sunlight from the plants in Afrekete's high windows.

I woke to her house suffused in that light, the sky half seen through the windows of thè top-floor kitchenette apartment, and Afrekete, known, asleep against my side.

Little hairs under her navel lay down before my advancing tongue like the beckoned pages of a well-touched book.

How many times into summer had I turned into that block from Eighth Avenue, the saloon on the corner spilling a smell of sawdust and liquor onto the street, a shifting, indeterminate number of young and old Black men taking turns sitting on two upturned milk crates, playing checkers? I would turn the corner onto 113th Street toward the park, my steps quickening and my fingertips tingling to play in her earth.

*And I remember Afrekete, who came out of a dream to me always being hard and real as the fine hairs along the underedge of my navel. She brought me live things from the bush, and from her farm set out in cocoyams and cassava*—those magical fruit that Kitty bought in the West Indian markets along Lenox Avenue in the 140s or in the Puerto Rican *bodegas* within the bustling market over on Park Avenue and 116th Street under the Central Railroad structures.

"I got this under the bridge" was a saying from time immemorial, giving an adequate explanation that whatever it was had come from as far back and as close to home—that is to say, was as authentic—as was possible.

We bought red delicious pippins, the size of French cashew apples. There were green plantains, which we half-peeled and then planted, fruit-deep, in each other's bodies until the petals of skin lay like tendrils of broad green fire upon the curly darkness between our upspread thighs. *There were ripe red finger bananas, stubby and sweet, with which I parted your lips gently, to insert the peeled fruit into your grape-purple flower.*

*I held you, lay between your brown legs, slowly playing my tongue through your familiar forests, slowly licking and swallowing as the deep undulations and tidal motions of your strong body slowly mashed ripe banana into a beige cream that mixed with the juices of your electric flesh. Our bodies met again, each surface touched with each other's flame, from the tips of our curled toes to our tongues, and locked into our own wild rhythms, we rode each other across the thundering space, dripped like light from the peak of each other's tongue.*

We were each of us both together. Then we were apart, and sweat sheened our bodies like sweet oil.

Sometimes Afrekete sang in a small club farther uptown on Sugar Hill. Sometimes she clerked in the Gristede's Market on 97th Street and Amsterdam, and sometimes with no warning at all she appeared at the Pony Stable or Page Three on Saturday night. Once, I came home to 7th Street late one night to find her sitting on my stoop at 3 A.M., with a bottle of beer in her hand and a piece of bright African cloth wrapped around her head, and we sped uptown through the dawn-empty city with a summer thunder squall crackling above us, and the wet city streets singing beneath the wheels of her little Nash Rambler.

There are certain verities that are always with us, which we come to depend upon. That the sun moves north in summer, that melted ice contracts, that the curved banana is sweeter. Afrekete taught me roots, new definitions of our women's bodies—definitions for which I had only been in training to learn before.

By the beginning of summer the walls of Afrekete's apartment were always warm to the touch from the heat beating down on the roof, and chance breezes through her windows rustled her plants in the window and brushed over our sweat-smoothed bodies, at rest after loving.

We talked sometimes about what it meant to love women, and what a relief it was in the eye of the storm, no matter how often we had to bite our tongues and stay silent. Afrekete had a seven-year-old daughter whom she had left with her mama down in Georgia, and we shared a lot of our dreams.

"She's going to be able to love anybody she wants to love," Afrekete said, fiercely, lighting a Lucky Strike. "Same way she's going to be able to work any place she damn well pleases. Her mama's going to see to that."

Once we talked about how Black women had been committed without choice to waging our campaigns in the enemies' strongholds, too much and too often, and how our psychic landscapes had been plundered and wearied by those repeated battles and campaigns.

"And don't I have the scars to prove it," she sighed.

"Makes you tough though, babe, if you don't go under. And that's what I like about you; you're like me. We're both going to make it because we're both too tough and crazy not to!" And we held each other and laughed and cried about what we had paid for that toughness, and how hard it was to explain to anyone who didn't already know it that soft and tough had to be one and the same for either to work at all, like our joy and the tears mingling on the one pillow beneath our heads.

And the sun filtered down upon us through the dusty windows, through the mass of green plants that Afrekete tended religiously.

I took a ripe avocado and rolled it between my hands until the skin became a green case for the soft mashed fruit inside, hard pit at the core. *I rose from a kiss in your mouth to nibble a hole in the fruit skin near the navel stalk, squeezed the pale yellow-green fruit juice in thin ritual lines back and forth over and around your coconut-brown belly.*

*The oil and sweat from our bodies kept the fruit liquid, and I massaged it over your thighs and between your breasts until your brownness shone like a light through a veil of the palest green avocado, a mantle of goddess pear that I slowly licked from your skin.*

Then we would have to get up to gather the pits and fruit skins and bag them to put out later for the garbagemen, because if we left them near the bed for any length of time, they would call out the hordes of cockroaches that always waited on the sidelines within the walls of Harlem tenements, particularly in the smaller, older ones under the hill of Morningside Heights.

Afrekete lived not far from Genevieve's grandmother's house.

Sometimes she reminded me of Ella, Gennie's stepmother, who shuffled about with an apron on and a broom outside the room where Gennie and I lay on the studio couch. She would be singing her nonstop tuneless little song over and over and over:

Momma kilt me
Poppa et me
Po' lil' brudder
suck ma bones . . .

And one day Gennie turned her head on my lap to say uneasily, "You know, sometimes I don't know whether Ella's crazy, or stupid, or divine."

And now I think the goddess was speaking through Ella also, but Ella was too beaten down and anesthetized by Phillip's brutality for her to believe in her own mouth, and we, Gennie and I, were too arrogant and childish—not without right or reason, for we were scarcely more than children—to see that our survival might very well lay in listening to the sweeping woman's tuneless song.

I lost my sister, Gennie, to my silence and her pain and despair, to both our angers and to a world's cruelty that destroys its own young in passing—not even as a rebel gesture or sacrifice or hope for another living of the spirit, but out of not noticing or caring about the destruction. I have never been able to blind myself to that cruelty, which, according to one popular definition of mental health, makes me mentally unhealthy.

Afrekete's house was the tallest one near the corner, before the high rocks of Morningside Park began on the other side of the avenue, and one night on the Midsummer Eve's Moon we took a blanket up to the roof. She lived on the top floor, and in an unspoken agreement, the roof belonged mostly to those who had to live under its heat. The roof was the chief resort territory of tenement-dwellers, and was known as Tar Beach.

We jammed the roof door shut with our sneakers, and spread our blanket in the lee of the chimney, between its warm brick wall and the high parapet of the building's face. This was before the blaze of sulfur lamps had stripped the streets of New York of trees and shadow, and the incandescence from the lights below faded this far up. From behind the parapet wall we could see the dark shapes of the basalt and granite outcroppings looming over us from the park across the street, outlined, curiously close and suggestive.

We slipped off the cotton shifts we had worn and moved against each other's damp breasts in the shadow of the roof's chimney, making moon, honor, love, while the ghostly vague light drifting upward from the street competed with the silver hard sweetness of the full moon, reflected in the shiny mirrors of our sweat-slippery dark bodies, sacred as the ocean at high tide.

I remember the moon rising against the tilted planes of her upthrust thighs, and my tongue caught the streak of silver reflected in the curly bush of her dappled-dark maiden hair. *I remember the full moon like white pupils in the center of your wide irises.*

*The moons went out, and your eyes grew dark as you rolled over*

*me, and I felt the moon's silver light mix with the wet of your
tongue on my eyelids.*

*Afrekete Áfrekete ride me to the crossroads where we shall sleep,
coated in the woman's power. The sound of our bodies meeting is
the prayer of all strangers and sisters, that the discarded evils,
abandoned at all crossroads, will not follow us upon our journeys.*

When we came down from the roof later, it was into the
sweltering midnight of a west Harlem summer, with canned
music in the streets and the disagreeable whines of overtired
and overheated children. Nearby, mothers and fathers sat
on stoops or milk crates and striped camp chairs, fanning
themselves absently and talking or thinking about work as
usual tomorrow and not enough sleep.

It was not onto the pale sands of Whydah, nor the beaches
of Winneba or Annamabu, with cocopalms softly applauding
and crickets keeping time with the pounding of a tar-laden,
treacherous, beautiful sea. It was onto 113th Street that we
descended after our meeting under the Midsummer Eve's
Moon, but the mothers and fathers smiled at us in greeting
as we strolled down to Eighth Avenue, hand in hand.

I had not seen Afrekete for a few weeks in July, so I went
uptown to her house one evening since she didn't have a
phone. The door was locked, and there was no one on the
roof when I called up the stairwell.

Another week later, Midge, the bartender at the Pony
Stable, gave me a note from Afrekete, saying that she had
gotten a gig in Atlanta for September, and was splitting to
visit her mama and daughter for a while.

We had come together like elements erupting into an
electric storm, exchanging energy, sharing charge, brief
and drenching. Then we parted, passed, reformed, reshap-
ing ourselves the better for the exchange.

I never saw Afrekete again, but her print remains upon
my life with the resonance and power of an emotional
tattoo.

# Judith W. Steinbergh

## Porch Lovin

Down here layin low on the front porch, we imagine
it's private, a thin vine, a short fir, a lacy
balustrade. We are huggin it up under the sheet
and soon your friend is up as we knew all along
it would be and before I blink you're naked on the
porch, your freckles low under the street lamp,
your cock nodding stiffly in the warm air. Hello,
hello it might be saying to the Silvermans' daughter
just returning from the Cape, but it's too busy in
me now speaking to that other darkness, that other
warmth and the sheet, our excuse at decorum is
almost useless billowing and slipping off our skin.
I speculate on neighbors so respectable they
barely make love in their beds let alone down on
the porch only a wilted pansy patch from the curb.
Bullshit you say, they're all doin it in the dark
recesses of their respective porches while Phoebe
the old setter comes sniffin, all of us are sniffin
and lickin, there's fingers in every orifice. What's
the difference, we all speak the same language.
A door slams, a car starts, all is quiet on the street.
Our low moanin from behind the landscape gardening
could be anything, an aquarium with a faulty motor,
a foghorn gone berserk and recuperating in the city,
but it's not. I come, you come, tum de dum and I come
and once again voices in the street ho hum just
restin here down on the floor at 99 Evans a single
family residence the authorities nod, the folks in
the street applaud, we stand and bow both naked as
moths and flicker in through the screen trailing
sperm sweet sweet.

# Dorianne Laux

# The Laundromat

My clothes somersault in the dryer. At thirty
I float in and out of a new kind of horniness,
the kind where you get off on words and gestures;
long talks about art are foreplay, the climax
is watching a man eat a napoleon while he drives.
Across from me a fifty-year-old matron
folds clothes, her eyes focused on the nipples
of a young man in silk jogging shorts. He looks up,
catching her. She giggles and blurts out, "Hot, isn't it?"
A man on my right eyes the line of my shorts, waiting
for me to bend over. I do. An act of animal kindness.
A long black jogger swings in off the street
to splash his face in the sink and I watch the room
become a sweet humid jungle. We crowd around the Amazon
at the watering hole, twitching our noses like wildebeests
or buffalo, snorting, rooting out mates in the heat.
I want to hump every moving thing in this place.
I want to lie down in the dry dung and the dust
and twist to scratch my back.
I want to stretch and prowl and grow lazy in the shade.
I want to have a slew of cubs.
"Do you have change for a quarter?" he says,
scratching the inside of his thigh.
Back in the laundromat my socks are sticking
to my sheets. Caught in the crackle of static electricity
I fold my underwear. I notice the honey-colored stains
in each silk crotch, odd-shaped, like dreams. I make
the panties into neat squares and drop them, smiling,
into the wicker basket.

# Patricia McConnel

# The Triangle

Wolfgang's song eased itself into Elizabeth's sleeping consciousness and nudged her awake. She smiled and savored the melodic yodelings a moment before opening her eyes. Every morning began this way; it was without question the most pleasant moment of her day. Wolfgang was still a distance up the hill. She had time to get up and put on the tea water before he arrived.

Then she stood, still naked, at the French window, which was the principal reason she had rented this tiny studio apartment in an otherwise dark and filthy basement. The window began about four inches above the floor and stopped just below the ceiling; it comprised most of the outside wall of the room and gave Elizabeth a pleasant feeling of living outdoors without the discomfort of getting wet when it rained. Because it was a basement apartment Elizabeth could simply step out the window into a neglected and cluttered garden. In good weather, the window stood open all day and night, admitting moths, flies, an occasional bee, fresh air, and smells from the neighborhood kitchens and gardens. Neither she nor Wolfgang ever used the door.

After a moment Elizabeth left the window and wriggled back into her sleeping bag, arranged her pillow so that her head was just above the window sill and watched the stretch of fence where she knew Wolfgang would first become visible to her. She could measure his progress down the hill along the rickety fence tops by the sound of his voice—a liquid trill originating deep in the throat. She could hear many messages in the song: "I am such a magnificent fellow; this enormous Potrero Hill world of backyards and fence tops is entirely to my satisfaction and this is my kingdom; if there are any ladies around—well, here I am." It was a song of celebration, self-assurance, and contentment, and it made Elizabeth feel better about being in the world,

no matter what might have depressed her the day—or night—
before. It also was the song Wolfgang sang to woo his
ladies, and it pleased her to imagine that he sang it on his
way home to her, Elizabeth.

Wolfgang appeared on the segment of fence Elizabeth
was watching just as the first rays of sun spilled over the
backyard. "You old rascal; you certainly know how to time
your entrance." Wolfgang jumped down into the garden
and picked his way gingerly through the gravel, raising his
eyes now and then to look at Elizabeth in the window. The
singing stopped; he was home. He stepped through the
window and with a little hop was on the mattress, purring
and touching noses with Elizabeth. "Your breath is as fresh
as creek water, Wolfgang. How do you manage that when
you don't brush your teeth?"

He looked directly into her eyes, as he always did, and
once again Elizabeth was astonished at their intensity, the
bright metallic green with gold flecks, the enormous size of
them. This frank, confident, and absorbed staring made
her feel an intense closeness and communication with the
cat. How nice it would be to get a person to trust you
enough to stare unwavering into your eyes. But only little
babies and cats do that.

"Just a minute, old fellow. Let me get my tea and then
we'll settle down for our morning cuddle. Do you want
some breakfast?" Elizabeth put a Mandarin Orange Spice
tea bag in her giant mug; then she shook some Friskies in
Wolfgang's bowl. He sniffed them but did not eat. Instead
he rubbed against her legs, purring. "Your friends next
door have been giving you steak and shrimp again, haven't
they. They're going to spoil you so rotten I won't be able to
support you."

Elizabeth took her tea to the mattress. Wolfgang was
there ahead of her. "Get out of the way so I can lie down."
He stood in the sleeping bag, gazing up at her in blissful
anticipation. Elizabeth put her tea on the window sill, scooped
Wolfgang up, and lay down with her head propped up just
enough so she could drink her tea. She set Wolfgang on her
stomach, and he started kneading, preparing his place. "Oh,
God, Wolfgang, your claws! Jeezuz. Here." Elizabeth laid
him down by picking up his front legs and pulling them out
from under him. He didn't mind. He arranged himself into
his favorite position: all four legs spread to the side rather
than underneath him like most cats. The result was that he
and Elizabeth were pressed belly-to-belly—she had come to

think of it as Wolfgang's pancake hug. She loved the feel of his soft, warm, furry belly against her bare skin. It was sensuous, almost erotic. In this mood of total trust and surrender Wolfgang was a liquid cat; she could do almost anything she wanted with his body. She picked up one of his paws, held it to her nose, amazed again at the pleasant musky smell of his feet. "Mr. Funky Feet," she said to him. Wolfgang purred.

Wolfgang now lay with eyes half closed, purring so hard that he drooled. Elizabeth reached for a Kleenex, put it under his chin, and studied the intense rainbow of colors the sun brought out in each hair of his coat, much like the colors in an oil slick—bright, metallic, intense shades of red, blue, green, gold, and purple. These flecks of color only showed up in the sun, and were so tiny that Elizabeth had not noticed them at all for the first year of Wolfgang's life. Now the jewels in his salt-and-pepper coat absorbed her every morning while she drank her tea.

Wolfgang shifted his position a little, bringing her attention back to the feel of his belly on hers, and without thinking, she responded by lifting her pelvis slightly, as if to meet a lover. She smiled and wondered if Wolfgang had any erotic feelings for her, or if it was all innocent affection. "Oh, Wolfgang, if only we could." She scratched his head and smiled again as he responded with an expression of blissful idiocy.

The sound of a key in the door startled them both. Wolfgang bolted through the window, scratching Elizabeth's stomach as he sprang to his feet. Etienne stood in the door, grinning at her. "God, you look terrific lying there in the sun. How are ya, babe?" He crossed the room and knelt to kiss her. As he leaned over her, the zipper on his leather jacket dragged across her breast. His breath smelled of coffee. She pushed him off. "What's the matter?"

"Your jacket."

"Oh, sorry."

"Got up early; thought I'd come say good morning before I go to work." His hand caressed her stomach, moved up to her breast.

Elizabeth could feel a callus on Etienne's hand dragging across her skin like a pin. She shifted herself to sit up, pulled the sleeping bag up over her body. "Want a cup of tea?"

Etienne smiled. "I want *you*." He took off his jacket and lay down beside Elizabeth. He took the cup out of her hand

and put it on the floor; then he held her face in both his hands and kissed her softly. He smelled of Old Spice. "Etienne, I'm allergic to perfumes. I told you before."

"Oh, I'm sorry, I forgot. I'll go wash my face."

While Elizabeth waited she tried to control her irritation. She knew he came not just to satisfy his own desire, but to surprise and please her. How could she say no? How could she explain her irritation without making him feel she didn't like him, didn't want him?

He came back to the bed, naked and hard. With the finger of one hand he entered her; with the other he parted her labia, and he kissed and licked her clit—the only man she ever knew who did it right: softly, like a woman. Elizabeth felt that soft, hot melting that was so delicious, almost painful. He brought her just to the edge of sweet explosion, then moved so that his body was over hers, and his cock entered the melting place. "Oooooooh."

"That's my baby."

He stroked her slowly, moving his pelvis so that he got her from every angle—an artist. But as his passion grew he stroked harder and straight into her, deep, driving. Her own ardor fizzled and she felt pounded. Etienne was beyond noticing. She could feel him getting harder and bigger; his eyes were closed and his head lifted. He did not notice how passive she had become beneath him. "Are you ready, baby?"

"Yes."

He let go.

Etienne collapsed beside her, smiling and panting, his eyes still closed. Then he turned to her and lightly kissed her shoulder, her breasts. "God, you're terrific, sweetheart."

Terrific? It didn't matter whether she responded or not, then? Elizabeth could not believe he was so blind to how passive she had been. She moved her head so she could look in his eyes. He was lying on his side with his head propped up in one hand. With the other he was tracing the outline of her left nipple. He met Elizabeth's stare but only a moment at a time. He kept glancing back at his hand tracing the nipple, as if this were an important task requiring close attention. Elizabeth resolved to make him look at her, really look into her eyes, with the strength of her own stare. But he was absorbed in her nipple and his own thoughts and did not look back at her again.

She studied Etienne's body next to hers. He had a nice body, taut, not fat, not exactly muscular but trim, hard. Nice. Except the color of his skin, a Mediterranean olive with a greenish cast that Elizabeth thought looked sickly. His cock now hung limp and glistening with Elizabeth's juices, almost comical in its floppy state, one-third its size of a few minutes ago. A slight movement caught Elizabeth's eye; his balls were moving. "Why do men's balls do that?" she asked.

Etienne glanced down at himself. "I don't know. They just do. They have a mind of their own."

Elizabeth held a secret opinion that balls were the ugliest things she ever saw, shriveled and sparsely haired, stupidly undulating of their own accord and sticky to the touch, like a semibald sea slug. "Wolfgang has gorgeous balls," she said.

Etienne grinned. "He does? I never noticed."

"His belly is all creamy colored and so is his bottom, but his balls are chocolate brown. They stand out against his creamy bottom. They twitch from side to side when he walks. I like to watch him from behind. They look sassy."

"Are cats' balls furry? I can't remember."

"Yes. Furry and clean. Very neat."

"Before you tell me I have sloppy balls, I'm getting out of here. Liz, I know it's crude to make love and then jump and go, but I have to go to work." He put a kiss on each nipple and got up. "I'll see you tonight, okay? Tell you what, if you can stand it, I'll cook. How's that?"

"Okay."

While he washed and dressed, Etienne half hummed, half sang his old favorite Elton John song, "Rocket Man." Elizabeth was silent, staring into her teacup, turning it endlessly in her hands. She wondered if Etienne was conscious of the humorous irony in the title of the song, considering the last twenty minutes. At last he came over to the bed on the floor, knelt beside Elizabeth, and, laying a hand on her knee, said, "Honey, is something wrong?"

Elizabeth looked up and directly into his eyes. He immediately glanced away. What is this? How can you enter my body but be afraid to enter my eyes? Elizabeth felt a door close in her head. "No, I'm just in a quiet mood this morning. I'm glad you came." Oh, God, she thought. Why did I say that? Why do I always acommodate men?

"So am I. I'll see you tonight."

Elizabeth felt relieved when he was gone. And guilty. Etienne was such a nice guy, always thoughtful, really. Why be mad because he closed his eyes to what might be painful for him to see: that he had turned her off by forgetting—

what? Etienne was a sensitive, skillful lover, but there always arrived that moment, just before he came, when he lost his sensitivity, when he seemed to forget that she, Elizabeth, existed, when he withdrew from her somehow. Her response became unimportant; even her comfort was unimportant, from the way he drove into her at the end. He was performing a solitary, self-centered act. Masturbating. And it wouldn't have mattered what body was under him. But it's not that, really, thought Elizabeth, because if I'm honest I do the same thing right at the end. I forget him, all involved in my coming orgasm. Then she remembered the challenge she had issued for him to look her in the eye. That's what's bothering me, she thought. It's that he wouldn't look me in the eye. Silly. Nobody likes to look you straight in the eye. Except Wolfgang.

Elizabeth got up and stood in the window. "Wolfgang? Wolfgang! Come on, ol' kitty, he's gone."

Tonight, though, I'm going to ask him for the key back. No telling how he'll take it, but I've got to get my key back.

"Wolfgang! Kitty, kitty, kitty?"

# Marge Piercy

# Under Red Aries

I am impossible, I know it,
a fan with a clattering blade loose,
a car with no second gear.
I want you to love freely, I want
you to love richly and many
but I want your mouth to taste of me
and I want to walk in your dreams naked.

You are impossible, you know it,
holy March hairiness, my green
eyed monster, my luna-
tic. On the turning spit of the full moon
my period starts flooding down and you
toss awake. Sleeping with you then
is spending a night on an airport
runway. Something groaning
from the ends of the earth is always
coming down and something overloaded
is taking off in a wake of ashes.

We are impossible, everybody says it.
I could have babysat in bobbysox
and changed you. Platoons of men
have camped on my life bivouacking
in their war. Now, presumably both adults.
I am still trying to change you.
We are cut from the same cloth, you say,
and what material is that? A crazy quilt
of satin and sackcloth, of sandpaper
and chiffon, of velvet and chickenwire.

I love you from my bones out, impulses
rising far down in the molten core

deep as orgasm in the moist and fiery pit
beyond ego. I love you from the center
of my life pulsating like a storm on the sun
shooting out arms of fire with power
enough to run a world or scorch it.
We are partially meshed in each other
and partially we turn free. We are
hooked into others like a machine
that could actually move forward,
a vehicle of flesh that could bring us
and other loving travelers to a new land.

# Ai [*Florence Ogawa*]

## Why Can't I Leave You

You stand behind the old black mare,
dressed as always in that red shirt,
stained from sweat, the crying of the armpits,
that will not stop for anything,
stroking her rump, while the barley goes unplanted.
I pick up my suitcase and set it down,
as I try to leave you again.
I smooth the hair back from your forehead.
I think with your laziness and the drought too,
you'll be needing my help more than ever.
You take my hands, I nod
and go to the house to unpack.

I undress, then put on my white lace slip
for you to take off, because you like that
and when you come in, you pull down the straps
and I unbutton your shirt.
I know we can't give each other any more
or any less than what we have.
There is safety in that, so much
that I can never get past the packing,
the begging you to please, if I can't make you happy,
come close between my thighs
and let me laugh for you from my second mouth.

# Restoring Spirit

# Joan McMillan

# Stephanie

My daughter, born
when the broken claws of orchard trees
filled with green, healing themselves over and over
with the white and salmonpink smoke of blossoms

that time of year
when seeds and bulbs
tear new fingers greedily through the rained-on soil
as if to say
"There is no other ecstasy but this."

We named her Stephanie:
"a crown"
for the nine months
she lay cushioned by the garland of pelvis

for the fontanel, the entering-place of dreams

for my body stretched wide in labor to permit her crossing
skin of my self pulled taut the blood in my ears roaring
as music roars in a string of wire
named her in the belief
that the world might not end
that we should live forever

a promise
burning deeper than language, brittle and lovely as bone.

## Roberta Hill Whiteman

# Star Quilt

These are notes to lightning in my bedroom.
A star forged from linen thread and patches.
Purple, yellow, red like diamond suckers, children

of the star gleam on sweaty nights. The quilt unfolds
against sheets, moving, warm clouds of Chinook.
It covers my cuts, my red birch clusters under pine.

Under it your mouth begins a legend,
and wide as the plain, I hope Wisconsin marshes
promise your caress. The candle locks

us in forest smells, your cheek tattered
by shadow. Sweetened by wings, my mothlike heart
flies nightly among geraniums.

We know of land that looks lonely,
but isn't, of beef with hides of velveteen,
of sorrow, an eddy in blood.

Star quilt, sewn from dawn light by fingers
of flint, take away those touches
meant for noisier skins,

anoint us with grass and twilight air,
so we may embrace, two bitter roots
pushing back into the dust.

# Marge Piercy

# Snow in May

It isn't supposed to happen:
snow on the apple boughs
beside the blossoms, the hills
green and white at once.
Backs steaming, horses
stand in the crusted pasture
switching their tails
in the snow, their broad
flanks like doors of leather
ovens. We lie on a mattress
in the high room with no
heat. Your body chills.
I keep taking parts of you
into my mouth, finny nose,
ears like question marks,
fatfaced toes, raspberry
cock, currant nipples, plum
balls. The snow hangs
sheets over the windows.

My grandmother used to drink
tea holding a sugar cube
between her teeth: hot boiling
strong black tea
from a glass. A gleaming
silver spoon stood up.
Before we make a fire of
our bodies I braid my black
hair and I am Grandmother braiding
her graystreaked chestnut hair
rippling to her waist before
she got into bed with me
to sleep, dead now
half my life. Ice on the palm
of my hand melting,
so cold it burns me.

# Amber Coverdale Sumrall

# Siesta

Grandma's house has a green gate that opens on a court-yard with brick-red tiles from Mexico. Bright blue-and-yellow pots, filled with cactus, sit on the adobe ledges. Birds of paradise border the patio. Grandpa's hand-carved gourds, painted with Indian symbols for rain, hold mounds of walnuts, figs, and peaches from the backyard trees.

We sit in wicker chairs, in the summer sun, drinking Postum from tall orange mugs with wooden holders. I pretend it is coffee. I always feel like I'm on vacation when I visit, even though we live in the same city.

Grandpa leaves to work in his garden. When we're alone, Grandma tells me stories about her family. She's proud to be Indian. She's descended from three different tribes; one's called Mohawk. Whenever she says Mohawk, I think tomahawk. I know what a tomahawk is, I've seen them for sale in souvenir stores in Yellowstone National Park. Indians used to scalp white men with them. Grandma says tomahawks were the first axes. She says that if white men had minded their own business instead of poisoning Indians with alcohol, shooting them and stealing their land, the Indians wouldn't have had to scalp them.

She sighs, "You'll never find the truth in your school books, honeygirl. It's all been turned to lies. Same with religion. Got to look real hard for the truth nowadays."

Grandma calls me honeygirl. So does Grandpa. Every morning he gets up before dawn, to grind wheat in the basement for his breakfast. Grandpa cooks all his own meals. That's because he likes to eat his supper when most people have breakfast, and have milk and fruit in the evening. He even washes his dishes and puts them away.

Grandma and Grandpa love each other more than anybody I know. He brings her flowers from his garden and they hug and kiss a lot. I mean real hugs and kisses, not the

166

quick dabs my father gives my mother before he goes off to work. Grandma scratches Grandpa's back, too. Lucky Grandpa. Having my back scratched is just about my most favorite thing. Grandma says love is the most important thing in the world.

"That's why we're born, honeygirl," she says. "To learn how to love each other. And it takes all the time we've got. Some folks never get the hang of it."

We finish our Postum and Grandma says it's "siesta" time. She and Grandpa nap together every afternoon. Today she has promised to nap with me.

The house is cool and dark. I follow her into the spare bedroom and climb on the four-poster bed. Grandma doesn't look Indian; she looks like a gypsy. Her dresses all feel like silk; she wears scarves and bracelets, earrings and glittery brooches. I think Grandma is beautiful. Her dark braided hair is rolled in circles on the back of her head and held by two silver clips.

Grandma pulls back the white chenille bedspread, then the blankets. I take off my shoes and socks, jeans and shirt. She lets me sleep naked, says it's too hot for covers. I crawl across the bed until I touch the cool plaster wall, then lift the sheet over me. The cracked yellow window shade flaps in the afternoon breeze.

"Santa Ana's are blowing again," she says. "Wind's full of evil spirits. They make folks crazy." She chuckles. "Even spirits get to create some mischief now and then."

She slides her flowered dress over her head and lets her slip fall to the floor.

Grandma's huge breasts rest on her belly. Blue veins run through them like tiny rivers. I've never seen real breasts before. Mother hides hers. She says women are cursed because of Eve's sin with the devil, and that I'll find out for myself someday. She says I'll have breasts someday, too, but I don't believe her. I hate dresses and perfume and patent-leather shoes. Daddy says I'm a tomboy. How can a tomboy grow breasts?

Grandma rolls into bed with me. She is naked, too. "I thought grownups had to wear nightgowns or pajamas to bed," I tell her. "That they could get arrested for being naked."

"Someone's been filling your head with foolish notions," Grandma says. "I won't mention any names. Come close, honeygirl."

I snuggle next to Grandma, nestle against her warm breasts,

her soft round belly. She holds me, kisses my neck, then moves slightly away and begins to scratch my back with her long fingernails. I feel goose bumps all over my body. Her nipples graze my back. I want to touch her breasts, suck on the hard nipples.

She traces circles round and round with her fingers until I can barely keep my eyes open.

When I wake, Grandma is gone. I have to pee and pass by Grandma and Grandpa's bedroom. Their door is shut and it sounds like they are bouncing on the bed. I want to peek, but I'm scared. They are making strange noises that I've never heard before. I know what they are doing has something to do with Grandma's breasts. I just know it!

I go back to bed and pretend I am napping with Grandma and Grandpa. My hands find the safe, tingly place between my legs.

It is almost dark when I wake up again. The smell of stewed rabbit gets me up real quick. I put my clothes on and go out to the kitchen. Grandma and Grandpa are sitting in their bathrobes, smiling at each other. They are smiling and rocking in their rocking chairs, looking like they've got a secret.

"Supper's almost ready, honeygirl. I fixed your favorite: stewed rabbit and dumplings. And Grandpa made fruit salad for dessert. Are you hungry?"

"I'm starving!"

"Well, we all seem to have worked up powerful appetites," Grandma says. She winks at Grandpa, then at me.

"Powerful indeed," Grandpa says.

## Enid Shomer

# Hair

When I was small
long hair announced my sex
and braids were the way
it was kept

Now nights I let my hair out
like an animal that needs
to roam under stars
before I sleep

It has grown long
as an argument between us
You preferred it short,
manageable as a handful of coins

but it is abundant
as Italian money,
a basketful of lira
to trade for a loaf of bread

When I'm old
and my nightgown hangs
in hospital corners
from my bones

and my hair is confined
to a white plait,
I want you to remember
the black against your pillow,

how it tented your chest,
how it announced itself
like the presence of flowers
in a dark room

# Beth Brant

## A Simple Act

*for Denise Dorsz*

Gourds climbing the fence. Against the rusted crisscross wires, the leaves are fresh. The green, ruffled plants twine around the wood posts that need painting. The fruit of the vine hangs in irregular shapes. Some are smooth. Others bumpy and scarred. All are colors of the earth. Brown. Green. Gold.

A gourd is a hollowed-out shell, used as a utensil. I imagine women together, sitting outside the tepees and lodges, carving and scooping. Creating bowls for food. Spoons for drinking water. A simple act—requiring lifetimes to learn. At times the pods were dried and rattles made to amuse babies. Or noisemakers, to call the spirits in sorrow and celebration.

I am taking a break from my hot room, from the writing, where I dredge for ghosts. The writing that unearths pain, old memories.

I cover myself with paper, the ink making tracks, like animals who follow the scent of water past unfamiliar ground.

I invent new from the old.


Story One

*Sandra*

In the third, fourth, and fifth grades, we were best friends. Spending nights at each other's houses, our girl bodies hugging tight. We had much in common. Our families were large and sloppy. We occupied places of honor due to our fair skin and hair. Assimilation separated us from our an-

cient and inherited places of home. Your Russian gave way
to English. Your blond hair and freckles a counterpoint to
the darkness of eye and black hair massed and trembling
around your mother's head. My blond hair, fine and thin,
my skin pink and flushed in contrast to the sleek, black hair
of my aunts, my uncle, my father. Their eyes dark, hidden
by folds of skin. We were anachronisms . . . except to each
other. Our friendship fit us well.

We invented stories about ourselves. We were children
from another planet. We were girls from an undiscovered
country. We were alien beings in families that were "different." Different among the different.

Your big sister Olga wore falsies. We stole a pair from her
and took turns tucking them inside our undershirts. We
pretended to be big girls, kissing on the lips and touching
our foam rubber breasts. Imagining what being grown meant.
In the sixth and seventh grades our blood started to flow,
our breasts turned into a reality of sweet flesh and waiting
nipples. The place between our thighs filled with a wanting
so tender, an intensity of heat from which our fingers
emerged, shimmering with liquid energy, our bodies spent
with the expression of our growing strength. When we
began to know what this was—that it was called love—
someone told on us. Told on us. Through my bedroom
window where we lay on the bed, listening to the radio,
stroking blond hair, Roger, the boy next door, saw us and
told on us. Our mothers were properly upset. We heard the
words from them: "You can't play with each other anymore."
"You should be ashamed." "WHAT WILL PEOPLE THINK?"

We fought in our separate ways. You screamed in Russian as your father hit you with his belt. You cursed him,
vowing revenge. Your mother watched, painfully, but did
not interfere, upholding the morality of the family. My
mother shamed me by promising not to tell the rest of the
family. I refused to speak to her for weeks, taking refuge in
silence, the acceptable solution. I hated her for the complic-
ity we shared.

Sandra, we couldn't help but see each other. You lived
across the street. We'd catch glimpses of the other running
to school. Our eyes averted, never focusing. The belt marks,
the silences, the shame, restoring us once again to our
rightful places. We were good girls, nice girls, after all. So,
like an old blouse that had become too thin and frayed, an
embarrassment to wear, our friendship was put away, locked
up inside our past. Entering the eighth grade in 1954, we

were thirteen years old. Something hard, yet invisible, had formed over our memory. We went the way of boys, back seats of cars, self-destruction. I heard you were put in the hospital with sugar diabetes. I sent a card—unsigned. Your family moved away. I never saw you again.

Sandra, we are forty-one now.

I have three daughters.

A woman lover.

I am a writer.

Sandra, I am remembering our loss.

Sandra . . . I am remembering.

I loved you.

We have a basket filled with gourds. Our basket is woven from sweet grass, and the scent stirs up the air and lights on our skin. This still life sits on a table in front of our bedroom window. In late afternoon, the sun glances around the hanging plants, printing designs on the wall and on our arms as we lay on our bed. We trust our love to each other's care. The room grows heavy with words. Our lungs expand to breathe the life gestating in the space connecting your eyes to mine. You put your hand on my face and imprint forever, in memory, this passage of love and faith. I watch you come from your bath. I pull you toward me, my hands soothed by the wetness on your back and between your thighs. You smell of cinnamon and clean water. Desire shapes us. Desire to touch with our hands, our eyes, our mouths, our minds. I bend over you, kissing the hollow of your throat, your pulse leaping under my lips.

We touch.

Dancers wearing shells of turtles, feathers of eagles, bones of our people.

We touch.

## Naomi Clark

# The Ring-Necked Snake

Once, grubbing out stumps, you
gashed a snake—I want you to
remember. You brought it to me,
silver-gray with a coral belly, necklace,
smooth rounded jaw. The silver within
made an iridescence so deep—
and its black eyes—one of those nights
when, before we had a house,
from a rock on the cliff's edge
we watched the moon rise late,
turn the ridge-top silver-gray,
shadows of the lateral ridges star black,
the canyon's chaparral a paler wash.
We saw deer then, browsing on oak leaves;
raccoons silver and black moved from one
spot of light to another through leaves' shadows;
a fox watched us from another rock. The flesh
of the snake's side, torn, showed white.
The slow cold blood mixed with dirt.
The snake twisted, doubled,
redoubled its shining length,
gray over coral, coral over gray.
You put it in my hands.
Cupped against my breastbone I held it
till it lay quiet and still.
You cleaned the wound, led me
down the slope, lifted the stump.
We placed the snake where as it slept
the steel had caught it,
to die in its own place
all we could give.

*　　*　　*

A year later, working the firebreak,
You turned over a log,
called me to see a snake, silver-gray
with a coral belly, coral necklace;
where the gash had been,
a scar like braided leather, healed.
The snake coiled round my arm,
tasted the air as I lifted it,
ducked under my shirt,
climbed my breastbone.
You turned the log back; you'd leave it.
We placed the snake where a crook in the wood
made a door. You,
who when we came here feared and hated
all snakes, were not jealous.

## Jill Jeffery Ginghofer

# The Natural Lover

Moving slowly
into the morning,
I crunch through the debris
of the children's room,
draw back the curtains
and find myself staring
into the steadfast eyes
of a large owl
sitting on the lowest branch
of the Joshua tree.

I run out and stand
idolatrous before him
in the rain,
ridiculously unfeathered,
my outsize housecoat
flapping about me.
At last a sign, a portent,
the Gods have noticed my struggles.
He gazes over my head
oblivious as the film star
looking to the limousine
at the curb.

Schooltime, and the children
smile shyly,
slipping into the car
beneath the owl.
As we roll down the driveway
he lifts his wings wide
and, effortlessly,
silent as snow falling,
glides the curve of the earth

to a neighbor's roof.
I am relieved.
He has blessed us and
gone his wild way.

When I return
he is in the same place.
A thrill of dread runs through me.
What does he want?
My children are gone,
the hamster sleeps
in his ball of shavings,
the kittens beneath the bed.
Can he smell
my giant vermin blood?
Does he know
I can resist nothing that loves me?

I rush beneath him
shrinking from the claws on my back,
the beak in my clavicle.
All afternoon I rage through my chores,
a woman distorted,
glaring from windows.
Does he expect
saucers of skinned mice
outside the door every evening?
He'll have to realize
I can't take any more love.

Yet when
early dusk
the rain a fine drizzle
the tree is empty,
I feel a pang
the sense of blood organs.
Gone his spotlight on the
dark larder of the night,
the black air filling his wings.
I am left in the crowded gloom
palely turning within walls.

# Lynn Luria-Sukenick

# Do You Know the Facts of Life? (Quiz)

Sample question: *Did you ever, as an adolescent, want to kiss your own mouth in order to know how you felt to the people you were paired with randomly at parties, when the opposite sex still seemed as remote as Egypt? How many of you still want to kiss your own mouths?*

If you did well on the sample question you'll want to take the rest of this exam. Sample answers are provided to the following questions in order to keep you company in your ruminations and to give you encouragement if you hesitate or stray. A final score will not be tallied in this quiz.

1. *We all know that the origins of sexuality are in the family. Write a brief essay about sex in your family.*

Her mother, when she's very little, informs her that babies come from seeds. She inspects every flowerpot in the house to see if a brother or sister is on its way. Later her mother liberally expands the information but keeps a strict eye on her growing daughter. In fact, because of her mother's watchfulness there are many episodes in the girl's childhood of *feelie interruptus*. Billy Emerson's boy's breath two inches away in a tantalizing almost. Games of doctor with little red pills and white caps. And her mother popping up like a doll out of a Swiss clock, always, at the sexiest moment, calling, "Hi kids, milk and cookies!"

2. *What was your first sexual game?*

She is seven years old and she and Barbara Lombardi are on the porch with their clothes on playing a game they invented called Naked in Hell. They are pretending they have big firm shapely breasts like movie stars in 1940s sweaters but they are naked and in hell where it is all right to be fiendishly wicked and naked. There is no narrative line in this game (which is invisible to anyone observing them); the point is to set the scene and then feel the tension of the naughtiness, to delight in hours of tumescence and then at dinnertime run into their houses to be little girls in the bosoms of their families. This is the same year that Lana Turner, according to a Hollywood exercise coach, had a perfect body for one week, and four years before Barbara is sexually approached in their neighborhood by a stranger the police fail to apprehend. By then they are eleven years old and she has to walk Barbara home if it's after dark because she's the brave and untouched one. But on the way back, alone, she makes her repel-the-attacker face, grimace of a Japanese actor, while inside of herself she chants, "I'm plain, I'm plain, don't hurt me, don't hurt me," over and over, until she has reached the warm and extended light of her mother's window.

3. *Write an essay on sex and school.*

Richard Krebs, the sixth-grade bully, tells her he can see her when she takes a shower. Although she knows this is impossible she thinks he may have some apparatus, the kind boys invent and girls don't, that will allow him to see her, so she takes faster and faster showers. Then, apparently overnight, Jerry Smith turns from good boy into dirty joker, "How far is the Old Log Inn? Yuk yuk." She doesn't like the coarseness of the jokes, though she does enjoy the secrecy the jokes are told in. On the way home from school the girls run away from the boys so they can be caught (additional question: *When did your cleverness begin?*) and she looks forward to that from lunchtime until 3 P.M. One day Michael Garrison spreads the rumor that he saw under her skirt when it flew up, but she knows he didn't because he didn't mention the "Tuesday" embroidered in red against white cotton over her appendix. In any case, taunts are compliments in those early days, and the girls thrill to them because they are a sign of interest, an advance over being shunned. This is where confusion begins, and these divisions are reflected, finely honed, even in her recent dreams.

4. *Relate a recent sexual dream, or several recent sexual dreams.*

She has had two sexual dreams this week, one tantric and one horrific. In the tantric one she's sitting in the archaeologicalligraphy café with her lover, the sunshine streaming in on ferns and oak tables. There are ancient runes on the walls, the braille of shadows and light. She and her lover finger the runes for sexual instructions, which are instantly translated by their bodies into their bodies. In the horrific dream a karate expert chews up pieces of wood until he has crammed his mouth full of splinters. Then he leans forward to kiss her. She wakes up.

5. *Now see what connections exist between sex and sleep.*

She and her lover spend many days in bed making love eating leftover Chinese food playing backgammon eating pizza making love watching Busby Berkeley and *Black Orpheus* on the black-and-white TV he tells her the colors five days go by and he says, "Are you really going all the way into the kitchen? Let me go with you" reading her Zippy and *King Lear* playing guitar it is summer sultry a scrim of leaves outside the window they are singing endless duets of scat invented on the spot they make up a pastime called Scenes You Never Saw writing the erotic passages left out of the great novels they relinquish themselves to the heat by accident he knocks her earrings off in his passion it's all she wears he always finds them again and places them in her palm they worry they'll forget how to buy food go to the bank read a book call a friend you put your forefinger in he says and dial and *then* what she says then say hello he says  and then what their legs are gently pretzeled they can't get up they giggle they need a servant they are starving to death their bodies ache maggots are in the garbage hairs in the sink the daily papers accumulate at the door of the clapboard house the air-conditioning's breaking down his spinster cousin whose bed they are in comes back from vacation after they've gone and finds it clean but she has insomnia every night for a whole year.

6. *Explore the relationship between sex and insomnia.*

She has insomnia, so she's watching the Johnny Carson show. Joan Rivers is on, horsefaced, skinny, and funny. She was making love with her husband, Rivers says, when he said, "Say something dirty." She was immediately responsive: "The bathroom," she said, "the kitchen, the living room, the playroom." While she watches TV she thumbs through a paperback someone left behind, *The Coming Celibacy*. Edward, eight months celibate, says, "I'm much more sensitive to things now. For example, I can hear a lot better if there's something wrong with my car." On screen two puppets are enacting an adultery scene, the wife at home is being visited by the milkman. "I can't open the door in my underwear," she says. "You have a door in your underwear?" the milkman replies. "Let me in and I'll help you open it."

7. *Interview one or two of your friends on the subject of underwear.*

"I really like it," says Andrea, putting her feet up on the coffee table. "My all-time favorites were crimson silk with eggshell lace to be seductive for Ted before things got bad between us, then I gave up and wore flannel and wool. Girdles? I did wear a girdle for forty minutes in Shiraz. I had gotten really fat on pistachio nuts and could not get into this blue silk dress and Mother and Dad had to push me into her girdle minutes before the ambassador's party and then I got a stomach ache and had to go home and never wore one again."

While talking to Andrea she remembers her honeymoon in Paris, where a friend had warned her about a flourishing white slave trade in lingerie shops: middlemen would snatch you from the cubicle where you were trying on your *soutien-gorge* and sell you into a bordello in the Sahara. She was twenty, her fingers trembling; she fastened the garter belt made of slender strips of lace as her husband stood guard outside, the way he stood guard at the famous hairdresser's, keeping him from cutting more than an inch of her waist-length hair, the hair that was so often praised by the artists she posed for back in New York.

8. *Have you ever posed in the nude?*

She works as a model for a few serious New York artists and occasionally for a commercial artist. One night the commercial artist does a series of drawings he hopes to sell to *Playboy* of her reaching, twisting, dreaming into space, all very beautiful, really. It's nighttime, his studio is on the twentieth floor of an office building, luxe and quiet; dead cameras standing around on tripods, two enormous drawing boards, Cartier-Bresson photographs on the walls, humanized hi-tech. Everytime she takes a new pose he says, "Great! Great!" It is a strange experience to know that he sees far more in her than what, at that moment, she feels in herself. This, she realizes later, is exactly what it means to be an object. As he keeps busy with pad and charcoal it frees her to drift and dream. She stares for ten minutes at the face of a Russian woman in one of the photographs until she feels herself lift into an enlightenment she has never felt before. Years later she understands that even meditation has not given her that sense of stillness and of clarity. The artists are not predatory but, on the contrary, protective and fatherly. She feels the air on her naked body as they sketch an image of her onto the soft stretched canvas, and it is as if she is three years old and playing at the shore while her parents sit close by, laughing and eating sandwiches but keeping an eye on her, building her sense of who she is just by being there.

9. *Have you ever posed in the nude with your clothes on?*
He photographs her face while she's telling him a subtly erotic story. It looks like an ordinary picture when it's developed but it excites him every time he looks at it.

10. *Have you ever attended a pornographic movie?*
She and her husband are parting, a marriage of many years begun in Paris and ending in California, and spend their last evening together at the movies, a common practice among divorcing couples. With a sense of fitness and of humor they attend the program of historical comic erotic movies at the local art cinema, and her annoyance with the banality of those bodies using each other without emotion wins out over her terror and delight in seeing so much active flesh. At the break before the feature an attractive man sits down in the empty seat on her right. Her husband has left in order to go to the men's room. She asks the man if he saw the shorts. "No," he says, he came for the feature. "They were stupefying," she says. It is clear that he enjoys her use of the word *stupefying* and she enjoys his enjoyment of it. They chat a little. Her husband comes back and he and the man exchange mild but indescribable looks. When the lights go out she feels how fully the man fills his seat, and she leans slightly closer to him than to her husband as a symbol of her new life as distinguished from her old. The man moves a fraction closer, and she feels the density of the muscles of his upper arm next to hers. The entire movie is spent adjusting these fractions closer and closer, allowing them to be background to the film and then foreground, eclipsing the film, until at a certain point she and the man simultaneously feel a need to rest, and withdraw, like two sweaty people flung apart to cool after making love. She is surprised at how merry and comforted she feels: he has a solid body: it is very nice. She does not, however, have fantasies that involve sex with strangers. If she'd wanted to be anonymous, she wouldn't have said "stupefying" after all, a word that would set her apart from other people, especially in California.
*Reflect on your answers to the questions above and take a ten-minute break.*

\*    \*    \*

Begin again with some short answers:
11. *What is the opposite of an obscene phone call?*
It's a call where you breathe gently, surprise them with kindness, and hang up. A good thing to say is, "Everything you've done up to now has been just fine with me," or "You, too, will love again."

12. *What is your favorite advice-to-the-lovelorn column?*
She reads in Ann Landers's column a query it will take her at least twenty years to comprehend. "I'm worried," says the correspondent, "because I am pregnant by a man who has slept with so many women I cannot be sure he is the father of my baby."

13. *Now, at your leisure, notice what sexual associations cling to the objects that surround you. Or close your eyes and remember other objects and places you have, at some time in your life, charged with eros.*
Memory is itself sexual, a dionysian attachment to the past accomplished in the face of the scythings of Father Time. She closes her eyes and thinks of: nude beaches; the skin of birches; surfers taking a wave that will never return; damp heaps of russet leaves; *keep cooking till chicken falls off fork*; a willow tree that sinks to its knee as the light subsides; a chemise with green flowers swaying into ivory like the pattern on her grandmother's fine Victorian china, a pattern he liked, the edge of her hand in his mouth, the woods all around, half in darkness, then later the two of them spilled open like loosened yarn or the day she met him in winter sun she said my hands, they're cold, and he took them between his own steepled fingers, the delicious prestige of a first gesture.

*Now take a twenty-minute break. During the break, lie down, close your eyes, and imagine your own nakedness. Then, using only your imagination, paint your body until you are covered from the soles of your feet all the way up through your hair. Apply whatever colors seem right to you, by whatever means. When you are finished, lie quietly for a few minutes.*

14. *Having relaxed yourself completely, write an essay that is also a confession.*
A year before the divorce and after long consideration she took a lover—not the usual adultery (guilt, repentence, the stunned mate) but a passion undertaken with her hus-

band's tacit consent. In spite of that consent whenever her lover called she pulled the phone on its long cord into the walk-in closet and sat among the dresses and skirts and trousers to mute her conversation and to find the privacy she did not want her husband's voice, deep in her head, to encroach upon. Her husband had a suit he liked, a Pierre Cardin that hung in a zippered cover next to where she leaned against the wall to talk on the phone, and she would look abstractedly at the silvery printing on the case, CAR DIN, and think about the rush of traffic outside the hotel where she had last met her lover, and about the novel and graceful allegiances of his golden dreamy body. She would talk to him for hours and emerge from the closet dizzy with the murmur of their voices folded over one another, letting the murmuring seep into her as she lay on the bed in a stupor. One day she reached for her coat in the closet and realized that her dizziness was caused not by her lover's voice but by the mothballs nestled in her husband's suit, their cold insulting sweetness even now seeping into her nostrils and numbing her slightly. Her husband's cleverly accidental control of her while she talked to her lover made her feel she was losing the last of her power, and she decided finally that the marriage was over. The day she packed her bags, a month after she had broken up with her lover because it would be dishonorable to abandon one man simply to go to another, she scooped the mothballs out of the zippered case and replaced them with a dozen candy Easter eggs she had bought that morning at Woolworth's when she was buying her luggage tags. She neatly arranged the yellow-and-violet eggs under the knife-creased and impeccably silent suit. And then she bit a hole in it.

15. *Follow this confession with a consideration of the spiritual side of things. What real or imagined encounters have you had with sex gods or goddesses?*

It's November 1, All-Souls' Day, the day, she thinks to herself, that the dead come back in the form of candy. She's at the local sweet shop, eating chocolate because she's lonely, when suddenly a vision appears. She always hallucinates a little if she eats a lot of chocolate and today she sees a woman in a preshrunk pink punk T-shirt and sheepskin chaps with a banner across her chest that says SEX GODDESS except the s seems to have fallen off. "I'm on a lecture tour," the goddess says. "I talk about how in the fifties people lay together like flounders and flopped up and down. In the sixties sex was based on political values; polyg-

amy echoed communal action. In the eighties everyone carries the burden alone. So promiscuity—from which the word
*prom* was taken—is—"

At the word *prom* a taffeta gown materializes, with a
pretty woman in it. "This is Pam," the goddess says,—"former
prom queen and pom-pom girl."

"Hiya," Pam says, "I hear you're getting divorced. Well,
honey, you're gonna be lonely. Eat that chocolate. How will
you ever live without a man, and I'm telling you, the men
out there are all too young, too mean, or married. You'll be
singing the blues," she says, and she sashays out humming
an old tune in 4/4 time, "If you don't like my sweet potato,
why did you dig so deep?" The ex-goddess shrugs, and,
shrugging, vanishes, chaps first.

16. *Write an essay on sex and solitude.*

She decides to prove the prom queen wrong and pro-
ceeds to lead a balanced and ascetic life, no chocolate. After
several months of this, however, she suddenly loses her
tranquilty to a lust that her laws against the young, the
mean, and the married will not allow her to satisfy. The
man dazzles her—red satin flash and life in the f-lane,
twenty-four hours a day. Why does she always fall for actors
and musicians, the strutting mimes and mummers, the brag-
ging drummers, men dependent on the vulgarisms of amps
and artificial lights, when she should be drawn to sonnets
and starlight? Violations of good taste have such appeal for
her that she wonders whether desire is only a state of
disorientation, a matter of breaking sober habits so deeply
ingrained that their very disruption seems erotic.

She falls into a state of sexual dyslexia: reading the Bible
for courage she understands it to say that Job is afflicted
with sore balls; taking her minerals in the morning she
finds a sodomite on the label where dolomite should be.
Hours are lost in fantasy. Finally she imagines going to visit
Herbal Cowboy, a healer, making a long trek through the
redwoods, home of hippie witches in their covens hovering
over their ovens and caldrons, to his shack in the moun-
tains, where he mixes a concoction and writes a prescrip-
tion. Her cure, he says, lies in dreaming the same dream
night after night, a dream in which she is scrubbing down
the steps of the Philadelphia Museum of Art. Eventually the
lust will disappear, provided she avoids looking inside the
museum—the Kandinskis have a certain bright diaphanous
thrust and shatter that might disturb. He also gives her a

pass to Wet World, where, having misread "groupers" as "gropers" and then as "groupies" on the giant fishtank plaque, she decides to soothe herself with mammmals instead.

She stand at the rim of the porpoise pool and one of the porpoises surfaces and puts his head close to her hand. She strokes his head and his back: it's like petting a giant olive. Intelligence always arouses her sexually, and the porpoise is no exception. She looks into his little eyes and feels herself getting turned on by his brain capacity. The porpoise is attracted by the sheen and shimmer of the satin cowboy shirt she is wearing, and he inches closer, his long nose touching her waist, as if he understands her human silliness and shine. She envisions how lovely it would be to swim with him, speaking in whistles and rusty hinge noises, clicks and pingings reverberating through her whole being, touch and sound indistinguishable in the echolalia as they plunge again and again below the mirror of silver waves.

After a day of these fantasies she goes to sleep and she dreams, not about the flashy man who inspired her lust, but about the porpoise. He speaks to her in playful swoops of freshness and rebounds of shyness, his body saying, "Swim with me! Swim with me!" As they swim, the water brilliant and quiet, he nuzzles her, the dark blue depths widening under them. And then, in the voice of a creature who now, involved, fears their differences, who cannot cross a border without vanishing, he says, "Let me go, for the day breaketh," and she lets him go, instantly, and wakes up feeling very clear, her eyes full of tears.

17. *You have almost finished the exam. Conclude it by sitting quietly in a lotus position. Close your eyes and contemplate the ten thousand sensuous things in the physical world. Don't tally your score.*

Notice the white throat of an iris, the quiver of emerald hummingbirds, the rolling gold hills of California summer studded with live oaks. (*What do you consider the most voluptuous season?* Don't rest with the obvious. Maybe it's the late yielding light of autumn, the intimacy in that clarity, the sharpness of light that brings everything closer.) Consider the texture of thin silk velvet, consider the scent of star jasmine, Billie Holiday's voice, any serious tenor saxophonist playing "Body and Soul," Edward Weston's nudes, Georgia O'Keeffe's orchids and lilies. Consider your childhood, the shapes of light in the room, the attentions and rhythms of speech, the fluxes and cuttings, the touch. This is the paradise where generosity begins. Swim with me, swim with me. These are the facts of life. Now, come to your senses.

## Susan Lysik

# Afternoon Poem for a New Lover

A conspiracy of doves and crickets
warms the mind,
while behind the long white shed
the willows lull softly,
teasing the insides of my wrists.
The silhouette of pines,
a dark and steady murmur
against the sun,
anchors me in the dusky heat.

Your animal breath
splits this body open,
skin curled back,
wantonly revealing the heart.

My vulnerable joy, flat and
pure as an altar cloth embroidered
with exquisite silence and pain,
could unravel with one
misplaced
sigh.
I lie mute and foolish,
overwhelmed by acceptance
and again
I marvel
at my capacity for renewal.

## Ellen Bass

# If You Want Me

you must approach
quietly as a doe
to the river for her evening drink
you must be slow as the
ripening of wood
with the patience of a village of weavers
bringing into being one perfect carpet

if you touch me
all the tenderness
of fathers watching birth
must pass through your hands
and you must enter softly
as one day slips into the next
through a long summer of sunny afternoons

if I cry, if my sorrow is not more dear
than oceans of dolphins in the orange morning waves

if you will not lavish me until my body
like a dying fish, gives up
and I swim like I have flown in my dreams

if you are saving something
if you have not
made up your mind
do not come to me

for I have been wounded
I am a lioness, I am
no longer young

# Maureen Brady

# Care in the Holding

Laura waited nervously while the woman filled out the contract for the rental car. "Two-seater okay?" she asked.

"Sure," Laura replied, confused about the question, which barely touched down in her float of a mind. What was she renting—a motorcycle? Minutes later, she found herself checking out the two-seater—indeed a car—a sporty Ford with bucket seats up front and a long hatch in back. Placing her directions on the other seat, she headed for the Bay Bridge, for her rendezvous with Chana, whom she was picking up at cousin Richard's in Berkeley Hills. Her mind printed an image of Chana—brown eyes with a sparkle in them, soft cheeks, sweet smell—and her heart sent a streak of excitement straight down her gut and into her loins. She'd been sitting on this excitement a whole month, since the hike they'd taken back East, which had tripped off a great glow in her heart.

She stopped in the hills when she sensed she was nearly there and tried to gather herself. Prepare. For what? She *knew* it would be good. She *knew* they liked each other. She *knew* the day on the mountain had felt like magic and they were the same two women coming together again. Breathe, she said to herself. She took ten long, deep breaths. On the tenth she realized she hadn't even checked to see if the charge was correct before signing the contract for the car rental. She dug it out and looked and felt further confused because they hadn't filled in the charges. But, of course: they were waiting to see if she'd return it on time.

More deep breaths. She felt lightheaded, maybe hyperventilation. What will she be like? The streak of adrenaline in her gut again. The feel of her clitoris standing upright. Go on. Jump. The waiting has been long enough already.

She started up the car. The next left was Chana's cousin's street and time speeded up. She was at the door ringing the doorbell. The door was large, opened out. Disorienting. She'd pictured Chana receiving her, inward, with the opening of a door, but now this door. What?

Chana pushed it open, came out herself with the door and gently hugged Laura, who was near to fainting. Chana radiant, wearing red, her eyes friendly, her short dark hair started down over her forehead, then curled back. She invited Laura in. Laura smiled yes, speechless, Don't ask me to talk. Chana took her to the back porch where cousin Richard and friend were sitting. They showed off the hummingbird at the bird feeder. The flutter of the hummingbird's wings felt like the stir inside her chest. The house was built on the side of a hill and the porch felt as if it was suspended in air. She glanced at Chana, caught the intensity of her beauty, felt as if the house was going to slide down the cliff. Said to herself: Keep breathing. Said to them: "Exciting to live here. You must feel on the edge all the time."

"I don't notice it at all," said cousin Richard, oblivious to the intensity of her feelings.

Chana took Laura to show her the bathtub she'd luxuriated in that morning. Once in the bathroom, she kissed her. Laura held Chana's head, held their cheeks together, and began to feel recognition from the last time. Her heart was pounding. She felt the ways they were strangers acutely, and wanted to hold their bodies together until they knew all the connections that were there.

"Let's say good-bye to my cousin and go," Chana said. He wrote out directions to the Richmond Bridge. Chana seemed composed, able to follow the directions. Glanced occasionally at Laura, flirting with the sparkle in her eyes. Laura went closer to the edge of the porch, looked out over the long view, but she still couldn't look down.

They left. They got lost on the first turn but drove on somewhat aimlessly. "What's your take?" Laura asked Chana.

"I think this will get us there."

"I like the way you follow your instincts," Laura said, going on down through Berkeley, feeling both cocky and lost. They were getting to know each other the same way. Laura alternated between feeling confident with that instinctual plane, which was restoring a kind of spiritual faith in her, and feeling a stranger, both to herself and to Chana. What if they were going blocks and blocks in the wrong direction? She wanted to be at the ocean, out of the car. She wanted to be where they could hold each other. Still she was glad to have the mission of driving. Needed time to establish a sense of Chana in the real flesh, not fantasy, before they made love. They had written sweet and tender love letters for the past month. Encouraging words, sharing of fragments of their lives: food tastes, books enjoyed, excitement about the work each was doing at the moment. Laura was having the good fortune of writing at a West Coast artist's retreat while Chana had been home in New York finishing a book she'd worked on for the past year.

From the moment she arrived in her retreat studio, Laura had noticed that the bedroom alcove was more fit for romance than for thinking up stories. The king-size mattress on the floor was made enchanting by the way two walls of windows wrapped around it. Outside, the branches of an oak tree reached in close to the windows. The patterns of the leaves, black at night, had a dreamy feeling. In the moonlight they lost their distinct edges and became blots placed in some mysterious order. They offered an entirely different impression, green, in the mornings. She had loved sleeping there, how the view helped her juxtapose the two different realities—the dream reality of night and the waking into a gentle California green. She woke with a kind of relaxed openness she hadn't experienced in herself for a very long time. And it was in that openness she yearned to wake and look upon Chana's sleeping face next to her. She wanted that openness, that wonder she had seen in Chana's eyes as they pulled back from kissing up on the mountain and looked each other full in the face.

They had crossed the bridge and were headed for the coast when they came into a misty fog. This was Laura's first time seeing it like this. The other times she'd driven up Route 1 she'd seen that magnificent long view of the rugged shoreline from the headlands. Now the fog closed around them and even when she knew they were near the ocean, she couldn't make it out. She'd only imagined bringing Chana here to the long view. Taking her by the hand and leading her down to a quiet spot on the hill and watching her take it in. The view awesome as the strong feeling that traveled breast to breast when they held each other. Now what? Chana took her hand and kissed it softly, then held it to her own heart. Laura smiled, warm inside. Scared, too. Who was Chana? Who was she? Why were they feeling so much while knowing so little about each other? She darted looks at Chana, but the curving road required her attention. Next time she saw a place to pull off, she did. Said Let's go down the hill a little and see if we can hear the ocean.

They both got out. Laura stretched, releasing some of the tension. It took a second for her to realize she was standing still, it was the car that was moving. Rolling backward. She ran for the door and hit the brake. Embarrassed at her driving ineptitude, she turned red. "You're distracted," Chana said, coming around. Laura put the car in park and pulled hard on the emergency brake, then laughed. "The navigator will have to see that the car is not left in neutral." Chana pulled her out and hugged her and kissed her. "Lucky we weren't on a big hill," she said.

They moved down to a point where they could see the waves crashing in on the rocks below. First they sat huddled close, as they had on the mountain, and kissed, smelled each other's hair, felt the deep magnitude pulling between them. Then they lay down. The fog created a room for them. They couldn't see the road or the sky. Sometimes they could see the ocean, sometimes not, but always they could hear its rhythm. They held each other and rocked together. "How I've longed for this," Laura whispered. "I know. I know," Chana replied. Their lust flushed their faces as they lay side by side, the full length of their bodies pressed close. The fog provided privacy. The room it made for them was impersonal, without decoration. It had no square corners, no flat walls. It moved in close. A gentle kiss grew into deep passion. When they looked again, the fog had thinned and the room expanded.

Laura felt one with her body and with the cliff they lay on. Her hand moved slowly up and down, charting the soft contours of Chana's body, remembering the curve of her back from the last time. She followed the line of Chana's firm thigh and pictured the gracefulness with which she would run, as she had the day she'd flown out to California while Chana had been running the women's half-marathon.

Chana pressed her pelvis closer and Laura'a lust peaked in response, sending charges like lightning, sharp through her body and back to Chana. She was breathless, delirious, joyous. Chana murmured how she loved her smell, rolled on her back, and Laura rolled with her so she was on top. Laura pressed into her, tasted and smelled Chana's neck, and inhaled deeply of the moist ocean air. She felt the hummingbird stir in her chest while her cunt both beamed a radiant heat and received the hot waves of Chana's sexual energy. Suddenly she wanted her naked. She wanted to be inside her, feeling the moisture she knew was there, wanted to have her own self known that way, free of the covering and constriction of clothes, but she knew this, just as it was, a kind of bliss, deserved its full due. Like a rose opening to full bloom, beautiful in all its stages, it had a timing all its own. She arched her head back and saw in Chana's face a desire that matched hers. How expressive her face was, how its movement reminded her of the waves below. Desire charging, cresting, then ebbing back as her closed lips fell into a quiet smile, broadening her face. Time was no more distinct than the boundaries of the room—seemed long if Laura thought of how much she was alive for each one of these minutes, short in the sense that there was no more waiting, waiting was over.

They stopped in a small beach town for coffee before going on to Laura's studio. Chana did most of the talking. Laura had trouble taking in the words or being verbal herself, though she wanted to make herself known this way. She had the precipice feeling again, like she'd had on Richard's porch, just from sitting across the table from Chana. She found her beauty so striking she was surprised the other people in the coffee shop were acting as if it were an ordinary day and not noticing that this clear-eyed, extraordinary woman was sitting across from her, sipping coffee and radiating joy. She went to the restroom and confirmed in the mirror that, sure enough, it *was* possible to see the radiance that she was exuding, as well. Her eyes looked bluer, her hair looked redder. Her skin looked soft and clear, ruddy and inviting. Warmth pulsed in her and she felt an openness that brought her in close to her own essence.

When they got to the studio, she still felt this closeness, but also the strangeness of the place, hers but not hers, a gift for the month, and the strangeness of their not knowing each other's homes. She led Chana around, pointing out the skylight at the peak of the building, the deck, the small kitchen, the charming bath. Still holding her hand, she led her down the two steps to the bedroom alcove. She fell onto the bed and leaned back, gazing out on her familiar and favorite view. "Come." She reached toward Chana, who stood smiling, then came down next to her. "It is paradise," she said, her voice almost husky. "You weren't making that up."

"Especially now, with you here, it is," Laura said.

Then they held each other and Laura's breath went away. She had to gasp for it somewhere under the lust. She felt the firmness of her own body as well as Chana's as they held tight. It was dusk and Chana's face was so wonderfully variable in that light. Sometimes soft with pleasure, sometimes scared, sometimes suffused with passion—all looks welcome to Laura as they reminded her of the complexity of her own feelings. She wondered, if they truly were strangers, why did their bodies seem already so well acquainted. More than acquainted, as if they'd been waiting and yearning a long time for this meeting.

They kissed deeply. Laura rolled on top. Chana put her hand at the base of Laura's spine and began rocking her back and forth in a gentle rhythm, and Laura felt the sweet warmth growing in her cunt. She ran her fingers through Chana's hair, held her lovely head, and loved the rhythm they both followed then. Chana pulled their shirts up enough so their bare bellies were touching and the warmth spread more fully to there. Laura felt their belly skins kissing—soft coverings overlying those guts pitched high with risk. She rose to take her top off and helped Chana pull hers off as well. Then they lay breast to breast and felt that warmth course through their chests. Laura cupped one of Chana's breasts in her hand and nuzzled down and tongued the nipple and watched it come erect. When she leaned back to look at Chana's face, Chana admired her breasts, saying they were perfect. Laura murmured her response. They rolled so that Chana was on top. Chana built on the same gentle but spunky rhythm. They built but did not come. What Laura needed for orgasm was no greater intensity than what they had already created; it was the building of trust. To feel the care behind Chana's caresses. And to trust that care.

Laura was raw in places, thin skinned in her recent healing from the breakup with her lover of seven years. It had been four months since she'd left their home, their bed, many more months since they'd been really alive, sexually, with each other. She remembered times when they'd put great effort into making love and she'd stayed for a long time on a brink, almost coming off that edge, but not quite, not quite able to. She remembered after her father died, when she came back home from the funeral, how she felt so alone. Bess didn't seem to really be there. She was, but she wasn't. Laura didn't seem able to ask her for what she needed. More holding. More care. More care in the holding. Bess was still depressed herself from having lost her job, and Bess came from a family where death passed in silence, feelings held in. So Laura had gotten to this brink and stayed there, knowing if she came it would be with a burst of tears, that her pleasure was enfolded deeply by her grief. Sharing the pleasure when she was not able to get the care seemed a betrayal of her body. And her body, often truer to her than her mind, balked. "It's okay," she'd told Bess. "We don't have to be so goal oriented." But Bess became reluctant to initiate sex with her, and this at a time when she wanted Bess to do the reaching out.

Chana on top of her was so much closer to her own size than Bess, who had been a good deal heavier than she. This position had always verged on feeling stifling to her with Bess. She felt a wave of her freedom and a joy at having made this choice. The wave brought her back to the glow in her belly, in her loins. At the same time, she felt tears very close to her pleasure. Chana was rocking her again and she felt comforted by this. The rhythm was right for her. How did Chana know to make it that way? Laura looked again to take in her face. Sweet, soft, full of mystery. She also has memory, she thought. Of what? Of whom? Where did this bonding, this movement toward intimacy take her? Her concentration was strong, she was all there, deeply inside her body. She called Laura's name. She said You, you, and Laura was wakened further by the call.

They stopped to kick off their pants, and then coming together again was like another new meeting. Like when the door opened out and Chana came with it. Like when they first lay on the cliff and held their bodies full length. Their bellies and breasts, their lips and cheeks came back together, familiar, still new but knowledgeable, warmed to each other. Laura put her thigh between Chana's and felt the softness of the skin that pressed her own. She felt the moisture of Chana's cunt and the beam of heat that burned out from her. She held still because the feeling inside her was already so full and she just wanted to feel it. A deep satisfaction with the awakening of all of her senses, her cells. She breathed in the sweet odor of Chana's neck, squeezed her own thighs and felt the heat coming out of herself. She reached to feel Chana's cunt. So nicely risen, soft and full like a bread with good yeast. Her finger slipped on the wetness as she explored. She felt both nervous and exhilarated, like nearing the peak the first time she climbed a new mountain. Would she be lost? Would she be found? Hearing Chana's response, she knew when her touch was right. She slid into Chana's vagina, a close cave, warm and moist and soft as velvet. A home. A mystery. How perfect that vagina felt and how forceful was its very being. Like the tide they'd felt while lying in the fog. She wanted to look, and did. She pulled away from Chana and ran her fingers up the path between the lips of the vulva and saw how pink she was. "A beautiful pink garden," she murmured. Her own excitement was increased by her words. She was expressing herself in a way she rarely had before. It was a new way of being active, of putting the feelings outside, between them, instead of tucked up close to her heart in a bundle the other would have to slowly work to penetrate. A garden was a place to grow in, a place of wonder. The wonder of growth. These caresses were the seeding of a love that might grow between them.

Chana pulled her back to a long body embrace, breast to breast. She held Laura tight around the hips and Laura felt the energy build heat in her belly. She felt the waves of Chana's energy driving her own higher and higher. She felt her heart so full of feeling. This woman was a stranger, yet she knew her. The whole month following their hike in Woodstock when they were separated, she'd felt Chana's presence very close beside her. A loving presence like a guardian angel. She'd felt her in that very bed, and ached with wanting to have her physical presence there.

Chana on top, raised herself up. She was radiant. Her dark eyes were joyous. Her dark hair stood up from her head and Laura ran her fingers through it. She kissed her breasts, her belly, as she moved down to Laura's cunt. There she became the explorer, parting Laura's lips and outlining the area gently with her fingers, then licking her. Kissing her. Sucking softly on her clitoris. Laura kept her hands in Chana's soft hair to anchor herself as she rocked her pelvis. She felt vulnerable with the absence of Chana's chest against her own, with the open air embracing her there instead, but she could feel love in Chana's mouth on her if she allowed herself to feel there between her legs. It was hard for her to take attention, to allow full attention concentrated on herself when she was not in the process of actively giving. But she talked to herself then: Said Take it. Let her love you. Let her find her own pleasure in this. Trust. The receiving required more trust for her than the giving. When she was able to concentrate on the feeling of Chana's giving, she glowed inside and moved her pelvis in response in a way that welcomed Chana's loving. She felt very full. She was on the verge of orgasm. She was on the verge of tears. What would it mean to cry in this woman's arms the first time they'd ever made love? She did not come. She did not cry. Chana came back to hold her full length, her lips next to Laura's ear. Spoke in her soft voice, which had been arousing Laura for a month on the phone, "I want you to come."

Laura's lust peaked at this spoken desire. "I'm moved by the way you touch me, the way you kiss me," she said, knowing as she released these words, they would take her past the tears.

"You can feel that . . . and still come," Chana said with quiet assurance.

"What about you?" Laura asked.

"I'm easy," Chana replied.

Laura felt the jets of adrenaline shooting from her heart to her belly. She felt her desire growing deeper, like a powerful undertow. Growing stronger and hotter as Chana's invitation ran in her mind. She reached down between them and spread both their lips so her clitoris pressed directly into Chana's, and moved against it. Chana whispered sweet words in her ear. Sometimes she couldn't make them out, but she could feel the care in them, the concentration. This was Laura and Chana together. Their histories were in them, all of the lovemakings of the past, but this now *was them*. Laura whispered Chana's name. She let her mind go. She was her body. She was the fire and the spirit that moved inside her. She rode it. She had been a long time waiting. Then she tripped off the edge and gasped and felt the glow spread inside her, like a sun coming out strong from behind a cloud. She moaned her pleasure. She felt the tenderness of Chana's arms around her. Her breath came quieter as she lay with her gratitude for the way this was possible, for the miracle of it, for the miracle of this woman, Chana.

Chana proved her ease. She moved with a confident connection to her body. She built, then stopped still for a moment, savoring some place she had reached she did not want to pass. Then she moved again. She was calling Laura's name, she was speaking to her cunt. Laura looked at her face—so full, so fine with desire, it fired her. Then Chana's breath turned to cries, each breath was a cry, each cry had an echo. Each echo touched Laura's heart. She held her. She held her. She was so happy to be holding her.

## Abby Niebauer

# To the Angel

. . . you touch so blissfully because the caress preserves.
"The Second Elegy," Rainer Maria Rilke

What I longed for was your hands
all over my body, everywhere your light
fingertips brushing away
the sheen of decay that had settled
on my skin. Wherever
you touched me I lived
in your fingers, the whorls
on the tips as you carried me
into the next hour, the next day.

The line of your jaw is still plain
to these fingers that traced
the bone. Perhaps you hold
someplace in your palms my forehead,
the curve of my back.

I wanted you to cover me
with your hands as if
you were a sculptor
releasing me into my true form,
as if you were a god building me
out of clay, to be a long time
perishing, so newly formed
and handed over to morning, lingering
these months on my lips.

## Heather Grey

# Elizabeth and William

William washed her gently, kissing the inside of her thighs and then turning her to one side to gaze at her buttocks. They were as full and round as before and with two dimples at the top. As he kissed them he remembered the times he had rubbed himself against them. Now he pulled her backward toward him and then let her go as he remembered the powder. He had every intention of getting her wet again, but the feel of the talc was good and it was important to keep her skin smooth and dry.

Elizabeth was now unable to move without some difficulty and needed support to avoid falling, so it was necessary for someone to be with her on the nurse's day off. The family came on Sunday; William took Thursday. He dusted powder into his hand and began to massage her. His hands moved further up her body under her gown into warmth. As he touched her breasts lightly he felt the nipples harden under his fingers. He stood up and took off his suit coat to avoid getting the white powder on the sleeve. Upstairs he could have risked getting undressed, but the sun room was just off the living room; if the nurse had returned unexpectedly he could not have dressed quickly enough.

William bent over and rolled her from her side onto her back, pulling the coverlet over the lower part of her body. This was the first spring day, and he was used to keeping her from being chilled. She smiled, looking at him with a mischievous dare, half taunting and half victorious. The jacket she had chosen for him that day was silk, sent from Paris by an earlier lover who had hoped to win her with expensive gifts.

He pressed his face into its cool smoothness, breathing deeply the scent of rosewater and feeling lost in the ruffles and folds as he rested his head between her breasts. She moved her hands and arms over his back, feeling the crisp cotton of his still starched shirt and the roughness of his wool vest. Moving her hands to his hair and beard, she touched his eyelashes, the bridge of his nose with its deep wrinkles, his eyebrows, and the lobes of his ears. Then she moved her fingers along the folds of his neck and over his cheeks as he lifted his head to take her fingers into his mouth. He sucked and bit them, feeling the softness of thin, almost translucent skin on hands as delicate as birds' wings.

Then he began untying the ribbons, moving his hands under her arms to catch her warmth and deeper body scent. He felt the smallness of her, his hands almost reaching the whole way around. Opening her gown, he stroked one breast with his finger before taking it in his mouth. As her breath quickened, she arched her body and lifted toward him, her eyes closed and her face turned away, coming closer and wanting him, but involuntarily pulling away from the sudden urgency. William removed the jacket and pulled her gown down around her waist. She felt exposed as he leaned over and began biting her neck and shoulders, rubbing his vest and buttons against her breasts. Moving the gown down farther over her hips, nibbling and sucking her belly as he went, he pulled off the coverlet and removed the gown. She lay quietly watching him as he looked at her. Slowly she opened her legs.

He covered her upper body with the gown to keep her warm, moved himself to the foot of the bed where he could sit comfortably and began stroking the bottoms of her feet. One by one he took each toe into his mouth and sucked it. Elizabeth's breath quickened and she uttered a small cry. He began massaging her deeply at the base of her thighs, opening them as far as possible, and then slipped his hands under her buttocks and pulled her to his mouth.

She lay in his hands, feeling the wetness of his tongue and lips, the soft bristle of his beard, the firmness of his fingers holding her locked against him. As her breathing became labored he quickened the motions of his tongue. When he felt her contractions begin he inserted his tongue, sucking gently until she cried out. Then he rolled her onto her side, her legs flexed, her buttocks fully exposed. Keeping one hand between her legs, fingers stroking alternately her anus and her vagina, he ran his tongue over her dimples and bit the fleshy parts of her hips and thighs. She felt the starched cotton cuffs of his shirt, the cool metal of his cuff links as his breath came warm against her ass. The contractions began again, slower and deeper.

Later she fell into a light sleep. She sensed him washing her again, the warm, soapy washcloth moving over her buttocks, into her anus and through her vulva. The she felt the towel, warm from lying in the sun, followed by the powder that he rubbed over most of her body. William bent his head to kiss her breast. She moved slightly, pleased by his continued interest, and smiled at his playfulness. He lifted her onto her pillow and watched as her head sank into the down. She was very light now and more the size of a child. When she was like this she had the innocence of a child as well, her earlier taunting and daring quieted. He hoped that when the end came it would come this way— with her drifting off, feeling treasured and wanted, after he had made love to her.

William had never mastered Elizabeth's hair. Soft gray tendrils were falling around her face; he had to be careful replacing the gown. Excuses could be made, but it would be better if the nurse found her the way she had left her. Elizabeth was light, but he was rather tired. He sat a minute to catch his breath, watching her in disarray, sleeping with complete abandon and trust, her breasts partly exposed; ribbons and lace intermingled against them. Pink, satin ruffles framed her face. He felt he had never seen her so beautiful or peaceful. The years had added wrinkles, she was pale and had more angles than when he met her, but she was still his Elizabeth.

As William rested, the tightness in his pant's leg became uncomfortable and he moved to adjust himself. It was only one thirty—plenty of time. Elizabeth never slept long. He went to the kitchen to make tea and then stood beside the window where he could see the patio where he and Elizabeth had spent their Thursdays last summer. In a wheelchair then, Elizabeth would position herself so her back was to the house next door and begin to undress herself as they talked, all the while pretending not to notice that her breasts were exposed. She was forever trying to figure out how they could arrange to make love in the hammock—even giving the nurse the evening off. Unfortunately (or perhaps fortunately, William thought) the neighbors had had a party on their patio the same night and the guests had stayed past Elizabeth's bedtime. William had had no intention of attempting anything in the hammock; he valued his back too much. But he had humored her. Elizabeth was always more passionate after planning forbidden and potentially chaotic encounters.

Their first relationship had been tumultuous and almost entirely sensual. She adored his uniform and he adored her spontaneity and freedom, particularly her freedom with her body. She teased him about his conservatism and he chastised her about her lack of responsibility. The relationship continued for several years until he was twenty-five. Then it ended for the same reasons it began: his uniform and her abandon. Neither of them could imagine homes and families based on the values of the other. He married Susan and moved away. She married a man named Alex. Through mutual, distant friends they kept track of each other's major life events: the birth of children and their graduations and marriages, the death of Susan and, eight years later, the death of Alex.

The first time he saw her again, sitting on the patio, she didn't get up but held out her arms to him, laughing. As he released his embrace she slid his hand unobtrusively along her breast. He could feel the soft warmth of her skin and was astounded that she could still do this to him. All he could think of was: Were her breasts bound by anything or were they completely free inside her dress? If he were closer could he just unbutton her and touch her as simply as he touched the china cup into which she poured the tea? He had not made love to a woman for almost ten years and thought that he might not ever again, yet now he was completely overwhelmed by thoughts of touching Elizabeth's body.

She had seduced him on the second visit. Setting the tea things aside, she had moved closer to him and leaned forward, letting him see the black lace slip barely covering her breasts. She had not taken it off, wanting his first kisses through it, wanting to feel the lace becoming wet under his mouth as he searched for her nipples, wanting the feel of his hands moving it over her hips and between her buttocks.

A few months later while they were at a party he had told her that he was becoming seriously involved with another woman and would not be seeing her again. She whispered in his ear, "If you move your hand under me no one will be able to see. You can touch me one more time." William could still remember the feel of the cool brocade upholstery and her warm, slightly moist crevice between the firm rounds of her buttocks. He had appeared at her home the next morning.

Now, turning away from the window, he needed to urinate and hoped that his erection had subsided enough to

avoid a painful release. He went into the hallway toilet and
positioned himself, trying to forget Elizabeth. He concentrated instead on the loose tiles under the sink and how
they could best be repaired. Then he stood for a moment,
feeling the warmth of his swollen testicles and flaccid, but
still tumescent penis, massaging it lightly, allowing it to
grow. She had been sleeping for almost an hour.

When Elizabeth awakened she looked down at her ribbons and lace and laughed. William hed left her just as he
liked her—accessible. Well, good enough. She stretched
and felt her body, clean and powdered and sensitive to the
touch where he had loved her.

She blessed the day she had bought this house. The
sunroom was one of the reasons, although she had not
known then that she would be spending so much time in it. It
had an old cobblestone floor and stone walls with almost
floor-to-ceiling, diamond-shaped leaded windows. Plants on
the window ledges flourished in the sun as she watched
from her not so cleverly disguised hospital bed. Since William was not able to lift her in and out of chairs or into bed
for her afternoon nap, the hospital bed was convenient.
Upstairs there was more privacy, but the lack of it added
charm, although William, not an adventurer in thought or
deed, probably would not agree with her. Perhaps some
day, if they had enough time with this new bed at just the
right height, they could try some of their old tricks.

She stopped her planning as William entered the room
with a paper cup in each hand and a bottle of Scotch under
his arm. He was still brown and muscular although he was
thinner and had a slight stoop. His hair was also thinning,
but he had developed a magnificent beard. She noticed that
he tired more easily and was not as sure of his ability to
handle her as she grew more dependent on physical support. Still, in uniform, he looked as if he were ready to
address the Joint Chiefs of Staff. Every detail was perfect
and appropriate: starch and creases. Even the paper cups
were somehow in keeping—the masculine no-nonsense solution, the only way to really drink Scotch. He had often
threatened to bring in the Scotch, but deferred to what may
have been her best interests. Perhaps he had decided her
best interests were too far to be served, and they should
damn the torpedoes and move full speed ahead. She pushed
the button to raise her bed to a sitting position. As William
helped her with another pillow, he quickly slipped his hand

into her gown. Elizabeth thought to herself: This is going to be no problem at all. He's still interested. His suit was tailored perfectly but not for an aroused state. She noticed that he sat down rather carefully.

She put down her cup and quietly offered to straighten his uniform; this was the first time she had suggested this since they had been at a family gathering, maybe posing for pictures, and she had decided that his uniform needed straightening. She had stood in front of him, her back to the others who stood in groups talking. With one hand she dusted and pulled at his uniform. With the other she rubbed him completely hard. His response had been immediate. He had frozen with embarrassment and confusion. She had then turned and stood in front of him while his arousal subsided, once or twice rubbing against him to delay his agony. They had never spoken of the incident. There was no use; Elizabeth was uncontrollable.

William stood near her so she could unfasten him without tiring her arms. Unbuckling his belt and loosening the top of his pants, she moved her hands as far up on his chest as she could, feeling his warmth under the starched shirt. As she lowered his zipper she could feel the heat and swell of him. She touched lightly, feeling the hard mounds held in damp cotton, and ran her hands over them. Then she moved him toward her head and adjusted the bed to the right height. She rolled onto her side with the help of his hand under her hip and moved closer, pressing her face into him, blowing gently, smelling his scent of spice.

Elizabeth felt his pubic hair through the thin cotton and the outline of his penis pressing against the gathers at the elastic band. She slipped her fingers up the leg and felt him hard, warm, and wet. As she pulled his pants down a little farther, she felt his resistance, his fear that they would fall, but she wanted her hand between his legs, cupping him, feeling the weight and size of him in her hand.

After moving farther back to stroke him and feel his heat, she pulled him closer so she could put her mouth on him through the cotton, smelling and feeling him with her tongue. She bit the shaft of his penis gently as far up and down as she could reach and felt him moving in rhythm with her biting. Then she pulled his waistband down quickly, feeling no resistance this time, and took his penis into her mouth, feeling the smoothness of him. He moaned and shuddered, placing his hand behind her head, the gesture as much a caress as a pulling of her farther onto him. He cradled her against him, one hand on her buttocks, massaging them almost involuntarily, and the other in her hair. She slipped his shorts farther down over his buttocks, kissing him and smelling the odor of him. Her mouth wet the base of his penis and she massaged it firmly.

Her hands tiring, she lay back, took his penis and rubbed it against the silk of her jacket, putting it inside against her breasts and wrapped her ribbons around him, resting and playing, while he grew harder; her fingers circled loosely around him, stroking lightly. He moved one hand to her breast, cupping it against his penis, while his other hand moved over her face and lips. She bit his fingertips and sucked them, moving her tongue along his palm, biting harder the fleshy pad at the base of his thumb.

Putting her hands into her gown, Elizabeth pressed both her breasts together against his penis and then pulled it out, enjoying the redness, the hard swelling. She kissed and bit him again, harder now, blowing as she breathed deeply and exhaled, finally taking it in her mouth and sucking. Determined not to let go she took it deeper and deeper. He began to move rhythmically, beginning the contractions, trying to push her away, reaching for the washcloth, but in his distraction coming in her mouth. She continued to suck and nibble until he was soft and small and he sighed.

As her hand still held him, William bent and kissed her mouth. The scents of roses and spices mingled with the strong sexual odors of their bodies. Exhausted, he sat and leaned forward, his face between her breasts, cradling her as she slept.

# Tess Gallagher

# Each Bird Walking

Not while, but long after he had told me,
I thought of him, washing his mother, his
bending over the bed and taking back
the covers. There was a basin of water
and he dipped a washrag in and
out of the basin, the rag
dripping a little onto the sheet as he
turned from the bedside to the nightstand
and back, there being no place

on her body he shouldn't touch because
he had to and she helped him, moving
the little she could, lifting so he could
wipe under her arms, a dipping motion
in the hollow. Then working up from
the feet, around the ankles, over the
knees. And this last, opening
her thighs and running the rag firmly
and with the cleaning thought
up through her crotch, between the lips,
over the V of thin hairs—

as though he were a mother
who had the excuse of cleaning to touch
with love and indifference,
the secret parts of her child, to graze
the sleepy sexlessness in its waiting
to find out what to do for the sake
of the body, for the sake of what only
the body can do for itself.

So his hand, softly at the place
of his birth-light. And she, eyes deepened

and closed in the dim room.
And because he told me her death as
important to his being with her,
I could love him another way. Not
of the body alone, or of its making,
but carried in the white spires of trembling
until what spirit, what breath we were
was shaken from us. Small then,
the word *holy*.

He turned her on her stomach
and washed the blades of her shoulders, the
small of the back. "That's good," she said,
"that's enough."

On our lips that morning, the tart juice
of the mothers, so strong in remembrance, no
asking, no giving, and what you said, this
being the end of our loving, so as not to hurt
the closer one to you, made me look to see
what was left of us with our sex
taken away. "Tell me," I said,
"something I can't forget." Then the story
of your mother, and when you finished
I said, "That's good, that's enough."

# Amber Coverdale Sumrall

## Out of Darkness

You thrash and moan
kick blankets off
your body arcs. . . .

Your father is dying
the bit of cold steel in his mouth.
He circles endlessly
in a corral of his own making.
You cannot show him the way.

I reach for you
you shiver, press against me.
I lick the salt from your skin
wrap my legs around you.
We ride out beyond the tremors.

## Abby Niebauer

# Afternoon I Almost Left You

I wanted the sky
to watch us make love
in these bodies where the spirit rages
against every separate thing
and longs for the time there was no time
when the flesh we lived in
covered us
with a single sheet.
And the sky rubbed against our window
and knew the everlasting glory
and despair of skin
while our bones went and stood
in a corner. Our flesh
so tender to the touch.
Just born, we were in a cradle.
Floating over us, clouds
we knew as Mother and Father
though we couldn't focus on their faces.
As the clouds changed shape
and flew over faster,
just in time
you returned to your body
and caught me.

# Jane Hirshfield

## Of Gravity and Angels

And suddenly, again,
I want the long road of your thigh
under my hand, your well-traveled thigh,
your salt-slicked & come-slicked thigh,
and I want the taste of you, slaking,
under my tongue (that place of riding desire,
my tongue) and I want
all the unnameable, soft, and yielding places,
belly & neck & the place wings would rise from
if we were angels,
and we are, and I want the rising regions of you
shoulder & cock & tongue & breathing &
suddenness of you
opening
all fontanel, all desire, the whole thing beginning
for the first time again, the first,
until I wonder then how is it
we even know which part we are,
even know the ground that lifts us, raucous,
out of ourselves,
as the rising sound of a summer dawn,
when all of it joins in.

# Biographies

**Janet Aalfs** lives in the Pioneer Valley of western Massachusetts where she is one of the head instructors of Valley Women's Martial Arts. Her poetry and fiction have been published in *Sinister Wisdom, Common Lives, Evergreen Chronicles, Lesbian Bedtime Stories, Red Flower: Rethinking Menstruation, By Word of Mouth: Lesbians Write the Erotic, Sojourner.* "I draw from the well of the erotic for strength in everything I do," she writes. "As a lesbian, I am aware of how much of myself has been feared, denied, and silenced. As a white, middle-class woman, I am equally aware of the privileges of acceptance, visibility, and comfort given to me by virtue of birth. I struggle against complacency in any form to create places for manifestations of the erotic to emerge, to become more fully and joyously myself."

**Deborah Abbott** lives in Santa Cruz, California, where she works as a psychotherapist. She is also a raft and kayak guide and the mother of "two beautiful sons." Her work has been published in *With the Power of Each Breath—A Disabled Women's Anthology, Red Flower: Rethinking Menstruation, Erotic by Nature, In Celebration of the Muse,* and in other sources. "I am a lover of women, of water, and of words," she writes. For her powerful definition of the erotic, please see the introduction.

**Elisa Adler** lives in the California Sierra Nevadas where she teaches English and Spanish and is assistant editor of the *Euphorbia Journal.* Her writing has appeared in various newspapers and magazines. "My sense of the erotic," she writes, "comes out in my poem. I don't think I could say it better."

**Ai** is of Native American, African, and Asian descent. She has published three books of poetry: *CRUELTY; KILLING FLOOR,* which was the 1978 Lamont Poetry Selection; and *Sin.*

**Cathryn Alpert,** a retired professor of theater turned writer, lives in Aptos, California, with two sons and a husband, Marco, whose intelligence, humor, and kindness serve as inspiration for many of her erotic tendencies, both literary and otherwise. Her stories, which have won national awards, have appeared most recently in *The Wittenberg Review, Rag Mag, Crazyquilt, Puerto del Sol, AIM Magazine,* and *O. Henry Festival Stories 1989.* She is currently working on a first novel.

**Renée Ashley** teaches writing in both New Jersey and New York. She received a 1989 Fellowship in Poetry from the New Jersey State Council on the Arts and won the 1988 Eve of St. Agnes Award for *Negative Capability,* the 1987 Ruth Lake Memorial Award from the Poetry Society of America, and the 1986 Washington Prize in Poetry. "Successful erotica must seduce the reader with the rhythms of sensual experience," she states. "It must woo her with the best-sculpted images that words can conjure, titillate her with the heat of the same, sweep her along in an unbroken stream of auditory sensuality through to its natural end."

**Margaret Atwood** was born in Ottawa, Canada, and currently lives in Toronto. She has published seven novels as well as books of short stories, children's books, poetry, and nonfiction, and has taught in universities throughout Canada. "As for my sense of the erotic," she states, "I'm not sure I have one detached from a surround of some kind. One might do worse than to quote Blake on 'the lineaments of satisfied desire.' "

**Ellen Bass** lives in Santa Cruz, California, with her partner, Janet Bryer, and their children, Sara and Max. She is a workshop facilitator for survivors of child sexual abuse and the coeditor of both *I Never Told Anyone: Writings by Women Survivors of Child Sexual Abuse* and *The Courage to Heal / A Guide for Women Survivors of Child Sexual Abuse.* She has also published several volumes of poetry, the most recent being *Our Stunning Harvest.*

**Sandy Boucher** is a fifty-two-year-old writer, teacher, and editor who is the author of *Heartwoman, Assaults and Rituals,* and *The Notebooks of Leni Clare.* "I don't think much about erotica," she writes, "perhaps because it seems such a natural part of life. And even though there are erotic scenes in my stories, I have only once sat down deliberately to write an erotic story."

**Maureen Brady,** author of the novels, *Give Me Your Good Ear* and *Folly,* and the collection of short stories, *The Ques-*

*tion She Put to Herself*, has been awarded grants from CAPS, New York State Council on the Arts writer in residence program, and Money for Women / Barbara Deming Memorial Fund. Currently she teaches writing workshops and is working on a novel. "I am interested in the kinship of spirituality and sexuality," she states, "and began writing more erotic and explicit lesbian sex when I realized that hiding its power (through silence) from others had the effect also of hiding it from myself. This writing has brought me both to the light and to the dark side, the discovery of being an incest survivor."

**Beth Brant,** born in 1941, is a Bay of Quinte Mohawk and a lesbian mother and grandmother. She is the editor of the anthology *A Gathering of Spirit* and the author of *Mohawk Trail* and *When I Kept Silence.* "Indigenous People have always known," she states, "[that] the power of the erotic is inseparable from the power of the spiritual. A woman standing on ground sights a bird. She is erotically moved by that bird because it transforms her to another place. The woman will go home and weave a story about the bird for her children, or a basket, and that erotic/spiritual moment is transformed once again. The bird will fly in search of food; it will rebuild its nest perhaps with a piece of thread from the woman's dress and that erotic/spiritual moment is transformed. Each spiritual being, the bird being and the human being, has altered its living."

**Anne Cameron** was born in Nanaimo, British Columbia, in 1938. She is the author of several novels, including *Dreamspeaker, Daughters of Copper Woman,* and *Journey*; a book of poetry entitled *The Annie Poems*; as well as other poems and numerous screenplays and short stories. "For me the erotic is not necessarily sexual but always sensual," she writes. "The strong hands of a woman carpenter, the muscles rippling in a woman's back as she hauls and stacks winter firewood, tanned skin dusted with garden dirt, the smell of moss and leaf mulch, blackberry juice staining laughing lips, the smell of the ocean after a storm, the strange unworldly hiss of drops of condensed fog as they drip from overhanging evergreen boughs."

**Naomi Clark** now lives in Port Townsend, Washington, after directing the San Jose Poetry Center, 1980–85, and teaching for many years at San Jose State University. In 1987 she held a NEA creative writing fellowship. She is the author of *Burglaries and Celebrations* and *When I Kept Silence.* Her poems have appeared in over sixty journals and periodicals. "My sense of the erotic does not include the pornographic," she states. "Rather it is an awareness, heightened at times by the grace of presence, of the holy in the relationship between spirit and mind and the things of this world—body, leaf, stone. It is the presence of the Great Goddess and of Eros, however he is known, in the abilities of us earthly beings. Ideally it may include joy, ribaldry, irreverence, but not cruelty."

**Lucille Clifton** teaches at the University of California at Santa Cruz and in Maryland. She is the poet laureate of Maryland and has been nominated for the Pulitzer prize in poetry. Her books include *An Ordinary Woman, Two-Headed Woman, Next,* and *Good Woman.* "The erotic is a natural part of my life," she states.

**Florinda Colavin** lives with her son and daughter, two dogs, and three cats in Santa Cruz. She drives over the mountain to San Jose each day to work as a therapist. She has been published in *In Celebration of the Muse, Lighthouse Point,* and other anthologies. "Having only begun to write after the birth of my daughter ten years ago," she says, "I have found that writing has given birth to my own inner voice. I believe that the core of this voice is the sensual-erotic self. The struggle to free this core is ongoing and central to my writing and to my life."

**Gina Covina** lives in Berkeley, California, where she follows her vocations as writer, artist, and publisher. Her books include *The City of Hermits* and *The Ouija Book,* and she has edited *The New Lesbians, The Lesbian Reader, and Amazon Quarterly, 1972–1975.*

**Rosemary Daniell** grew up in the Deep South where she still lives. She began writing at age eleven when she carved her name on her desk. Her books include two volumes of poems, *A Sexual Tour of the Deep South* and *The Feathered Trees,* as well as *Fatal Flowers: On Sin, Sex and Suicide in the Deep South* and *Sleeping with Soldiers: in Search of the Macho Man.* "I feel that I have been deeply influenced by growing up in a sensuous, yet at times repressive region," she writes. "The moist climate, the flowers, the Spanish moss dripping from the live oaks, even the bloody imagery of the Bible Belt hymns constantly battle the puritanical respectability aspired to by much of Southern society. This dichotomy creates a kind of constant subtext, an erotic energy, even an erotic obsession. But this is all beneath the surface: in my daily life I experience no separation between the erotic, the nonerotic."

**Flora Durham** lives in Oregon where she recently received an Individual Grant in Literature from the Oregon
Arts Commission. "I have a renewed commitment to the
powerful act of writing," she states. "The further we as a
people slip away from intimacy with our real surroundings
the more I feel compelled to tell the truth of it."

**Cerridwen Fallingstar** lives with her mate and partner,
Theo Bailey, and their son, Zachary Moonstone. She has
published over a hundred articles, poems, and stories in
various newspapers, magazines, and books and has completed her first full-length novel, *The Heart of the Fire.* "I am
a Priestess of Aphrodite as well as of the Caldron," she
states. "I believe that love is the basis of all spiritual trans-
formations. Sexual energy and spiritual energy are one
sacred flow . . . Eros is a child, innocent and pure, and a
God of love, winged with power, brilliant as sunlight. There
is no true eroticism without innocence and sacred power.
There is no true eroticism without love."

**Carolyn Forche** won the Yale Series of Younger Poets
award in 1975. She is the author of *Gathering the Tribes* and
*The Country Between Us,* the Lamont Poetry Selection in
1981.

**Tess Gallagher** lives in Port Angeles, Washington, and
teaches at the University of Syracuse, New York. Her books
of poetry include *Instructions to the Double, Under Stars, Will-
ingly,* and *Amplitude.* She has also published a book of short
stories, *The Lover of Horses.* "As for my sense of the erotic . . .
if you take away all shame and barriers to the clarity of
bodily knowing it's like entering the purr of a cat. There is a
sweet roaring in the hand and heart, for we like to be
stroked and to give over to the body its whole power so the
spirit hums."

**Jill Jeffery Ginghofer** lives in Santa Cruz, California,
with her husband and three children. Her poetry and prose
have appeared in *Cosmopolitan, Feeding the Hungry Heart, In
Celebration of the Muse, Matrix, The Sun,* and in other sources.
About the erotic she writes: "From the eyes in: Looking at
art, I feel intensely interested, moved, deeply excited, charged
with energy. From the skin out: Touching you, my hand
gliding over the warm, firm silk, through my fingers the
mystery, the blood and tingle of other. From the skin in:
My body touched, my sensing-self leaps to the defined bound-
ary, trembles where I meet space. Heat radiates from the
inside. Rapture: Almost as short lived as a butterfly, almost
worth dying for, and most women in male literature do."

**Heather Grey** is a professional artist and teacher who lives in New York. She writes, "I am interested in the sensuousness of the mature body over forty and the erotic possibilities of the person free of children, beyond striving for success and able to say this is it; I am damned well going to enjoy it! I am also interested in the issue of age because it is a necessary requirement, though not a guarantee, for developing the depth of intimacy required for such relationships."

**Jane Hirshfield** is the author of two books of poetry, *Of Gravity and Angels* and *Alaya*. She is also editor and co-translator of *The Ink Dark Moon,* a selection of the work of two women poets of ancient Japan. She has received a Guggenheim Fellowship, a Columbia University Translation Center Award, and other honors, and her work has appeared in *The New Yorker, The Atlantic, The American Poetry Review, The Paris Review,* and *The Pushcart Prize Anthology.* "All creativity is to some extent erotic," she states, "if by erotic we mean the arousal of heart, mind, and body toward some Other. The making of poetry that is explicitly sexual in subject is a way to touch, through content, on one of the central issues of human life: how we widen beyond ourselves."

**Zora Neale Hurston** was an outstanding novelist, journalist, folklorist, and critic. Between 1920 and 1950 she was the most prolific black writer in the United States. Her books include: *Their Eyes Were Watching God; Dust Tracks on a Road,* her autobiography; *Mules and Men,* and *Jonah's Gourd Vine.* "I love myself when I am laughing," she wrote. "And then again when I am looking mean and impressive."

**Yuri Kageyama** was born in 1953 in Aichi-ken, Japan, and grew up in Tokyo, Maryland, and Alabama. Her works have appeared in numerous literary publications including *Y'Bird, Breaking Silence: An Anthology of Contemporary Asian American Poets, Beyond Rice, Yellow Silk,* and *River Styx.* "The Japanese tradition unquestioningly accepts the erotic as an aesthetic," she writes. ". . . Women redefining our own sexuality is the object becoming the subject, along the lines of what's discussed in de Beauvoir's *The Second Sex.* Sexuality permeates our being, so much so that I feel that practically everything is erotic— the enjoyment of music, the entire reproductive process, everything that relates to creativity, life/death, and love."

**Maxine Kumin** lives in New Hampshire and teaches at Princeton University. She has published six volumes of poetry including *The Nightmare Factory, Up Country,* and *The*

*Retrieval System.* In 1974 she won the Pulitzer prize and was named consultant in poetry to the Library of Congress for 1981–82. She has also published four novels and a collection of short fiction.

**Dorianne Laux** was born in Augusta, Maine, during the early fifties and came west with her mother after "a particularly gruesome winter" to live in San Diego. She currently lives in Berkeley, California. "I try to get in touch with 'the erotic' on alternate Thursdays, after my daughter has gone to sleep," she writes. "Quite often it just doesn't work out. When in the span of a week the most erotic thing that happens to me is watching someone eat an eclair, I try not to think of it as a sign of age, but rather a deepening sense of maturity. My overall sense of the erotic is: anytime you can get it."

**Audre Lorde** is the daughter of Grenadian immigrants. Her most recent writings include a book of poetry, *Our Dead Behind Us*, a collection of essays, *Sister Outsider*, and the novel *Zami: A New Spelling of My Name*. It is her definition of the erotic that has inspired us and given us the underlying philosophy of this collection of writings: "When I speak of the erotic, then, I speak of it as an assertion of the life-force of women; of that creative energy empowered, the knowledge and use of which we are now reclaiming in our language, our history, our dancing, our loving, our work, our lives."

**Clarinda Lott** is an assistant professor of English at Towson State University and acts as a special consultant to Maryland Public Television. Her books include *Forms of Verse, British and American; The Pearl;* and *The Bone Tree*. About the erotic she writes: "It was part of my life way before puberty—in my mother's long, long hair and the Romantic variety of my writer-father's friends . . . a very positive force, especially in combination with my parents' amazing sexual candor (even by today's standards.) This early warm and healthy aura enabled me to survive some real horrors later on . . . to wait out a decade when I was ready to bag life's erotica and rediscover that sex can be warm, comforting, comfortable, and endlessly surprising."

**Lynn Luria-Sukenick** is on the faculty of the M.F.A. program at San Diego State University and has a private practice in writing and healing. She has published four books of poetry, including *Houdini Houdini*, and her short stories have appeared in *The Massachusetts Review, Fiction International, New Letters,* and *Yellow Silk*. "If I were writing an essay on eros," she says, "I would begin with this sentence: Eros is always political, always conditioned by the political—an ironic situation, because we think of intimacy as being our haven from the state. The reader can take it from there."

**Susan Lysik** was raised in Massachusetts and has lived in the Santa Cruz, California, area for over twenty years where she works in theatrical production. Her poems have been published in *The Wild Iris, Black Maria,* and *Plexus.* "If we give a reading in my neighborhood bookstore, will I have to follow someone who has talked about her Parts?" she asks. "If these things were meant to be public, we wouldn't have been given these black cardboard rectangles to hold up. I'm going to put mine over that delicate place at the inside of the elbow."

**Irene Marcuse** is currently living in New York City with her two-year-old daughter and works as a writer and editor after having such jobs as bartender, waitress, housepainter, carpenter, and wife to support her writing habit. She has had work published in *Moonjuice, Nimrod, Matrix, Dreamworks,* and *New Life News.* "The erotic lives in my fingers, my hands, my thighs," she writes. "It can only be felt, sensed, the melting of center, the leap in my throat. What is erotic is open, opening. Touch, the keenest of my senses."

**Patricia McConnel** is fifty-seven years old and lives in the Canyonlands of Nevada, where she divides her time between walking in the desert wilderness and writing. In 1983 she won a grant in literature from the National Endowment for the Arts. "I was in my mid-thirties before I allowed myself to understand that I can respond sexually to just about anything, even trees and the sun," she states. "Cats seem to me to be the most sensual creatures on earth. The psychiatric establishment considers this pathological and even has a clinical name for it: polymorphous perverse. *I* consider it being fully alive and responsive to the world and everything in it. I celebrate this blessing in my erotic fiction."

**Joan McMillan** was raised in Sepulveda, California, received her degree in literature from the University of San Diego in 1981, and moved to Santa Cruz, where she now lives with her husband and three children. Her poems have appeared in *Plainswoman, Porter Gulch Review, In Celebration of the Muse,* and *Lighthouse Point.* "My sense of the erotic has matured through my pregnancies and passages through childbirth," she writes. "A deepening awareness of my body's strength, power, and nurturing has helped me to heal and re-piece both self and spirit."

**Terry McMillan** lives in Brooklyn with her son, Solomon. In 1985 she won the Doubleday-Columbia University Literary Fellowship and in 1986 her first novel, *Mama,* was published. "I guess my sense of the erotic," she writes, "is words and images that swirl and melt softly inside me while I'm reading. Whatever is happening to a character makes me wish it were me; or at least conjures up warm feelings and causes me to reminisce about when I felt this plush inside, or pray that I will soon!"

**Maude Meehan** has been conducting writing workshops for women for several years in Santa Cruz and has been widely published in literary journals, magazines, textbooks, and anthologies. Her book of poetry, *Chipping Bone,* was published in 1988. She has also edited and published four anthologies of Santa Cruz women's poetry and is coauthor and editor of *Wheels of Fire,* a film script. "The erotic; the voluptuous involvement of the senses. The aphrodisiac of skin on skin. Certain music. Fierce wild wind and storm. Hot sun. Smell of new-mown grass, earth after rain, you. Snow falling silently, softly and a fireplace, burning. Melted chocolate on my tongue. That itch. Scratching it."

**Kathy Metcalfe** is a nurse, masseuse, and poet. She has been published in the book *Marginal and Footnote Poetry.* "I grew up in the rural Midwest," she writes, "where legs were 'limbs.' *Little Women* was acceptable reading for young girls and I became a composite of Jo, Meg, Beth, and Amy. It was years before I discovered the fifth 'little woman' —probably not mentioned in the book because Marmee was displeased with her behavior. This fifth sister refused to read *Pilgrim's Progress* and always kicked off her pantaloons. I'm quite fond of her."

**Deena Metzger** is a poet, novelist, playwright, and psychotherapist. Her books include *The Woman Who Slept with Men to Take the War out of Them* (a dramanovel), *Tree* (diary novel), *Looking for the Faces of God* (poetry), and *What Dinah Thought.* She is currently working on *Writing for Your Life: Creativity, Imagination, and Healing.* She is married, has two sons, and lives at the end of a dirt road with her wolf, Timber. About the erotic she states: "It is everything in service of the life force."

**Valerie Miner** teaches at the University of California, Berkeley. Her novels include *Winter's Edge, Blood Sisters, Movement,* and *Murder in the English Department.* She is also the coauthor of *Tales I Tell My Mother* and *Her Own Woman*. Her work has appeared in many journals. "For me erotic art involves tensions and pleasures—even issues and ideas," she writes. "It's not just a sex scene but an aesthetic that takes sensuality and sexuality into consideration at many levels and at many moments."

**Alice Munro,** while a Canadian writer, was born in Detroit in 1950. She has written short stories for *The New Yorker* and won the Canadian Booksellers Association International Book Year Award for her novel *Lives of Girls and Women*. Her other books include *The Moons of Jupiter* and *The Beggar Maid*.

**Abby Niebauer** had her first book of poetry, *Sun Rose*, published in 1985. About this volume, Galway Kinnell has said, "Her poems are faithfully, recklessly emotional and at the same time transcend and are spiritual." Her work has appeared in *Quarry West* and *Plainsong*.

**Sharon Olds** has published three collections of poetry: *Satan Says; The Dead and the Living*, which was the Lamont Poetry Selection of 1983 and won the National Book Critics Circle Award; and *The Gold Cell*. She teaches at New York University and at Goldwater Hospital, Roosevelt Island, New York.

**Marge Piercy** lives in Wellfleet, Massachusetts. She is the author of eleven volumes of poetry, the most recent being *Available Light*, and including *My Mother's Body; Stone, Paper, Knife;* and *Circles on the Water*. She has also published ten novels, including *Summer People, Gone to Soldiers, Woman on the Edge of Time, Small Changes, Fly Away Home, Braided Lives*, and *Vida*.

**Nancy Redwine** is a California immigrant living in Seattle, Washington, who calls herself a "self-educated, pagan, unemployed groundskeeper." A closet writer for thirteen years, she was published for the first time in the Autumn 1983 issue of *Yellow Silk*. "Tapping into erotica in my writing has been almost as gratifying as the erotica in my life (sometimes more so). Erotica is a celebration of sex as religion—all faiths: sex as high mass, tent meetings, and speaking in tongues. The erotic is a celebration of the force surging through our bodies, through this earth—that which keeps us wanting to live."

**Adrienne Rich,** who lives in California, is the author of numerous books, including *Snapshots of a Daughter-in-Law; Necessities of Life; Diving into the Wreck; Of Woman Born: Motherhood as Experience and Institution; Twenty-one Love Poems; The Dream of a Common Language; On Lies, Secrets, and Silence:*

*Selected Prose, 1966–1978; Your Native Land, Your Life;* and *Time's Power.* She has been awarded the first annual Ruth Lilly Poetry Prize and a Brandeis University Creative Arts Medal.

**Wendy Rose** was born in 1948 and is of Hopi and Miwok ancestry. She is a lecturer in the Department of Native American Studies at the University of California, Berkeley, as well as a poet and artist. Her work has appeared in *Akwesasne Notes, River Styx,* and *The Third Woman.*

**Helen Ruggieri** lives in New York and has written the book *The Poetess* and the chapbooks *The Poetess, Concrete Madonna, Rock City Hill Exercises, Walking the Dog,* and *River.* She has also been published in numerous magazines and anthologies. "An Encounter in Muse, PA" is a chapter from a yet unpublished novel that she began when she turned forty. About the erotic she says, "I'll pun and say it's felt knowledge rather than intellectual knowledge. I reveal myself most clearly in the fictions."

**Eva Shaderowfsky** lives in New York. In addition to writing short stories and criticism, she has been a photographer for the last twenty-two years. Her book, *Suburban Portraits,* a photo essay with words, was published in 1977. "About the same time," she writes, "I began a series of photos of the 'older' woman, which was spurred by a spread in *Playboy* called 'The Older Woman.' The oldest was thirty-two. The 'older woman' and the suburban woman as themes reflect my life and my concerns . . . The erotic cannot be separated from self-image, whether it is as a mother, wife, working professional, or as an aging sex object. It is an inextricable part of our sense of ourselves."

**Enid Shomer** is a poet whose most recent collection of poems, *Stalking the Florida Panther,* won the book prize of The Word Works. Her poems and stories have appeared in *Poetry, Ploughshares, New Letters, Midstream, The Women's Review of Books,* and many magazines and anthologies. "My sense of the erotic," she states, "is strongly linked to feminism and to my aesthetic. We live in a culture that considers the body—particularly the female body—as pornographic rather than erotic. I have enjoyed reclaiming my body in my sexuality and my work."

**Carol Staudacher** is a poet whose work has appeared in a variety of literary journals and anthologies, including *The New York Quarterly, Five Fingers Review, Ally, The American Writer, Primavera,* and *Lighthouse Point: An Anthology of Santa Cruz Writing.* She is also an author in the mental-health field and an editor. *"Real* eroticism is caused by love, given to love, enhanced by love," she writes. "To be capable of the erotic is to be willing to trust, to be vulnerable, to be inventive, and to be charmed and courted by the senses. When the pulse of life is honored as it trembles most tenuously in all living things, love will assume an imminence; then, and only then, is the redemption of the erotic possible."

**Judith Steinbergh** lives and teaches in the Boston area. She has published four books of poems, the most recent of which is *A Living Anytime*. She coauthored with Elizabeth McKim a book about teaching poetry: *Beyond Words, Writing Poems with Children*.

**Doreen Stock** a poet and translator, lives in California. Her works include *A Noise in the Garden*, poems of her own plus translations; *The Politics of Splendor*, prose poems and translations; *La Cuenta Mundo, Gabriela Mistral*, a translation; and *Five: The Transcript of a Journey*. "The erotic is a field of energy, profoundly tropical and mysterious, in which we regain paradise," she writes. "If love is not there we are robbed forever. In modern life it is deranged by machinery and mass culture, but if we remember, when 'touching fire,' that we are once more touching the sacred, then we are never lost."

**Amber Coverdale Sumrall** is coeditor of *In Celebration of the Muse: Writings by Santa Cruz Women*. Her poetry and prose appear in numerous literary magazines and anthologies, including *New Voices from the Longhouse, The Women's Review of Books, With the Power of Each Breath, Conditions,* and *Negative Capability*. She is currently working on an anthology of writings about menopause to be published by Crossing Press. "My sense of the erotic: great horned owls calling to one another at dusk, the voice of Ferron, the drums of Babatunde Olatunji, mangoes, figs, bearded iris, cactus flowers, patchouli, sweetgrass, ocean-polished stones in my hand, the taste of my lover's skin, Russian plum brandy, the baths at Tassajara, thunder, wind chimes, my cats, the courting dance of ospreys over water, the fluted song of the Swainson's thrush."

**Jan Sturtevant** graduated from UC Berkeley and earned an M.A. in literature from CSU, Stanislaus. Her poetry has been published in *Lighthouse Point* and *In Celebration of the Muse* and is currently expressing itself through her art quilts. "I believe the impulse toward another, toward true intimacy, is basic and essential," she states. "To lie down, naked and vulnerable, with another person, to open myself slowly, to partake as the other unfolds to me, these are basic human acts that connect me with the life force and with my own humanity. For me, this is a basic expression of the spirit and power of the erotic. Without it, I am diminished, stopped from expressing essential parts of myself. Words and gestures lie unused, accumulate like debris around my heart."

**Louise Thornton** was born on Valentine's Day, 1941, in a little town in Iowa. She lives in Santa Cruz, teaches in a community college, and is the coeditor of *I Never Told Anyone: Writings by Women Survivors of Child Sexual Abuse.* "The erotic is often utterly terrifying to me," she writes, "because acting on these feelings as a child led to what felt like abandonment by my mother. Nonetheless, eros seeks me out and persists with relentless energy until it flows out of my pen onto paper in scrawling loops and lines that calls itself writing. It also saves my life. When I am closed down, when I am isolated, when I am feeling hopeless, it washes over me in a wave. Live! it says. And I do."

**Patrice Vecchione** is the coeditor of *In Celebration of the Muse: Writings by Santa Cruz Women.* Her work has appeared in *Quarry West, Yellow Silk, The Berkeley Review of Books, Puerto del Sol,* and *Ikon,* among others. She teaches poetry and creative writing to children and adults in the Monterey Bay area. "My sense of the erotic: breath, touch, tongue, kiss, tease."

**Roberta Hill Whiteman** is a member of the Oneida tribe and teaches at the University of Wisconsin. Her volume of poetry is entitled *Star Quilt.* She has been published in *American Poetry Review, The Nation,* and the book *Carriers of the Dream Wheel.*

**Ann Zoller** has published two volumes of poetry: *Answers from The Bowing Moon,* which was a finalist in the University of Hawaii Pacific Poetry Series, and *New Pony on a Carousel,* the winner of the Pegasus Award for the best book of poetry published in 1983. She has been published in many journals and anthologies. "I love to be erotic and know the combination of my physical, emotional, and mental parts coming together, usually in intercourse to orgasm," she writes. "Eroticism is such fun! I also feel there is something quite wholesome in lust, feeling and experiencing the true emotion. To be erotic is to be free."